18/11/22 .

Please return or renew this item _New_ **East Sussex** County Council
by the last date shown. You may
return items to any East Sussex
Library. You may renew books
by telephone or the internet.

0345 60 80 195 for renewals

0345 60 80 196 for enquiries

Library and Information Services
eastsussex.gov.uk/libraries

D1350545

04268073

A 1950s Holiday in *Bognor Regis*

Sylvia Endacott
& Shirley Lewis

*To our parents, Lewis & Elsie Endacott and
Winifred & Norman Lewis, who always
enjoyed their holidays in Bognor Regis,
our adopted home town.*

First published 2014

The History Press
The Mill, Brimscombe Port
Stroud, Gloucestershire, GL5 2QG
www.thehistorypress.co.uk

British Library Cataloguing in Publication Data.
A catalogue record for this book is available from the British Library.

ISBN 978 0 7524 9912 3

Typesetting and origination by The History Press
Printed in Great Britain

CONTENTS

Acknowledgements   7

Introduction   9

Travel   19

Accommodation   31

Memories   49

Entertainment   79

East and West   111

ACKNOWLEDGEMENTS

We would like to thank the following organisations: Bognor Regis University of the Third Age (U3A) and the Shared Learning Project (SLP); West Sussex Record Office; Bognor Regis Local History Museum; also members from numerous U3A's.

Shared Learning Project members: Anne Barrow, Tim Eade, Richard Jeffery, Helen Krarup, Josie Landolt, Rodney Lees, Jill Wellman.

We also acknowledge the help given to us by Jane Barnes, Chris Burstow, Peggy Carrott, David Jennings, Sue Millard, Alan Readman and the late Sheila Smith.

We have received contributions and photographs (P) from: David Allam (P), Les Allatt, Eileen Anderson, Lyn Baily (P), Alan Binns (P), Paul Bignall, Margaret Bryant, Peter Burrell (P), Maureen Carter (P), Jill Chapman, Hugh Coster, Adrian Collyns, Mrs Cowell, Sheena Cribb, Sheila Dixon, Pauline Edwards, Barbara Eldridge (P), Kay Fall (P), Angela Ford, Tom Gillespie (P), Fiona Huntley, Anne Jeffery, Jenny Jennings (P), Clifford Jones (P), Ruby Knight, Josie Landolt, Roy Laing (P), Doug Law (P), Maureen Lord (P), Colin Manning, Anne Manville (P), Felicity Mills (P), Les Norman, Sylvia Olliver (P), Marilyn Paton (P), Charles Powell, Paul Rapley, Sue Reeves (P), Margaret Richards, Janet Rufey, Julie Scott, Ken Scutt (P), Jean Shearley (P), Paula Smith (P), Mary Streeter, Carol Tickner, Daphne Thomas, Gwen Twaites (P), Peter Tompkins (P), Liz Tribe (P), Val Warlow (P), Peter Williams, Brian Willis (P), Anthony Wills.

We have used images from our own archives, the Bognor Regis Local History Museum, the Gerard Young Collection, and the West Sussex District Council archives situated in the West Sussex Record Office. A number of photographs were also loaned from the Colin L.M. Bell collection, with associate information and assistance from Aidan and Hazel Bell.

Finally we acknowledge Anne Barrow, Jeni Pinel, Marjorie Spooner and Alan Warwick for proofreading and contents comments, and Ron Iden for his historical checks as well as general comments.

Cover images: Left – Esplanade Theatre postcard.

Right – Helen Scutt (centre) with her cousins, Hilary and Robin.

Back cover (left to right):   Hazel Macaulife, Malcolm Roberts, Roy Becker and his fiancée Kathy Richardson.

INTRODUCTION

Shirley and I have been involved in a number of publications over the years, dealing with specific subjects such as airfields, companies, people and the seaside, and relating to various times in the past. When considering local history it is understandable to think of it as 'days gone by', but when those days are part of one's own lifetime it takes on another significance altogether.

This book looks at our present home town, Bognor Regis, in the 1950s, although we did not move here permanently until the 1970s. The 1950s were an interesting decade; after the austerity of war, people welcomed the end of rationing. It was a period of change for everyone. As the decade progressed, people started thinking of holidays again, and in this publication we will look at how they travelled to their destination, whom they went with and where they stayed. On arrival what did they do, where did they eat and drink and who did they meet? In 2014 these may seem somewhat strange questions, but we think you may be surprised by the answers!

For the journey within this book we have taken the opportunity to speak with people who remember this decade, whether as holidaymakers or residents. We have read local and national newspapers and magazines of the 1950s and the annual Bognor Regis Urban District Council Holiday Guides. We teamed up with the Bognor Regis Branch of the U3A on a National Shared Learning Project and formed a team to look in depth at the subject. We have worked with the Bognor Regis Local History Museum, using their archives and research rooms; we have also worked with the West Sussex Record Office.

What were holidays like in the 1950s? People had, perhaps, a break of a week, or maybe two, at a favourite location. For many people, especially those with large families, there would be the opportunity of renting a caravan for a period, or staying at a bed and breakfast. In very popular holiday destinations, local people advertised that they would provide a bed and breakfast in their own home for a weekly rate; Sylvia's mother did this for a time in the 1950s in Plymouth. There were, of course, those who were only able to go to the seaside for the day, thus the day tripper became important to any resort.

When one looks around Bognor Regis in 2014, there is a Butlin's Holiday Resort, also some smaller caravan parks, and a number of hotels and guest houses, but it is a far cry from the profusion of hotels, caravan and camping sites and bed and breakfast accommodation that existed in the 1950s. Our expectations and needs have changed considerably over the last sixty years. We have moved from a time when only rich people had cars to one where it is not uncommon for several members in one household to each have a car. Many rented their homes in the 1950s, today home ownership is more prevalent. For many more people, holidays at home have changed to holidays abroad, weekend breaks and cruises.

In post-war Bognor Regis, the authorities and business owners realised that the holidaymakers and day trippers were returning, and so had to ensure there were services, activities and entertainment available to ensure a good holiday experience for everyone.

It is important to remember that the aftermath of the Second World War was still affecting daily life in the UK. Rationing was still in operation: petrol and soap rationing had only ended in 1950, identity cards were abolished in 1952 and in the same year the Utility Furniture and Clothing Schemes ended. Sweet rationing remained until 1953, when sugar rationing also finally ended after fourteen years. Not until 1954 did all rationing end.

In this book we have looked at a seaside resort in the 1950s through the eyes of holidaymakers, and also residents who spent their childhood in Bognor Regis. In a 1953 Kelly's Directory the Bognor Regis Urban District Council area is recorded as consisting of 2,695 acres of land with 352 acres of foreshore. By 1955 the population was recorded as 25,647 people. Much of the advertising for the town featured the phrase 'The Heart of the Sussex Riviera'.

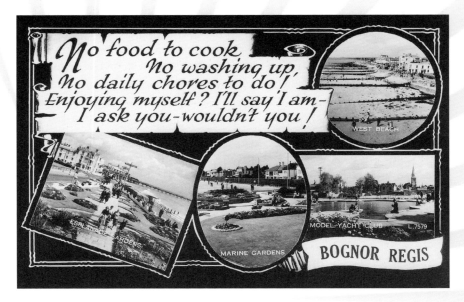

People speak of this time with such a depth of feeling that one gets carried along with their memories. We have added some historical facts and background information as necessary to complete these memories. It has not always been possible to place the very interesting pictures that we have been given into the text of the person who kindly supplied them; nor have we been able to use all the words and pictures you supplied and we hope you will understand our difficulty in deciding on the final content.

Sylvia Endacott & Shirley Lewis
2014

It has been interesting to read the newspapers of this era and to realise how similar the reports were. It is good to see how the press reported on our town.

The Times, 21 February 1951 – Popular Notions corrected:
'Taking the average for the whole year, the warmest places are the Scillies, The Channel Isles and Penzance. The Channel Isles enjoys the most sunshine, but Eastbourne, Worthing and Bognor Regis are not far behind.'

Early Days

I was born in 1952 and experienced my first Bognor Regis holiday in 1954. My grandmother used to rent both Valetta Cottages in Nyewood Lane for the month of July every year until 1962. She and her companion of the time took one cottage, and my parents and I, and sometimes my parents' guests, the other. The cottages then belonged to Mrs Newton and her daughter Iris, both teachers, who lived in London. The late Mr Newton had been a political journalist with the *News Chronicle*.

The cottages were very old fashioned with kitchen ranges, chenille cloths on the table and a noisy geyser in each downstairs bathroom. They both smelt slightly damp, but I loved them. They were my passport to the joys of the beach at Aldwick Road and visits to Pets Corner in Hotham Park and, until Butlin's came, the thrill of model railway trips on the flat lands at East Bognor.

My grandmother always hired two beach huts from the Grays who regaled me with stories of smugglers who had, they assured me, once lived at Valetta Cottages. They told me that there was a passage under the back garden in which contraband had been stored and a large number of ghosts lurked. Certainly the cottages had once housed a pig-farmer called Greenwood and my parents and grandmother often commented that they could smell bacon curing. So a culinary rather than a smuggling spirit was abroad in Nyewood Lane in the 1950s.

Beach life involved fishing for shrimps and crabs in the broken wreckage of the Mulberry harbour*, sandcastles and swimming. The hot summer of 1959 had the best swimming and beach life, although my grandmother always insisted

*Authors' Note – the wreck of a concrete Mulberry Harbour section which broke loose in a storm prior to being towed across the Channel on D-Day 1944.

David Allam aged 6 years.

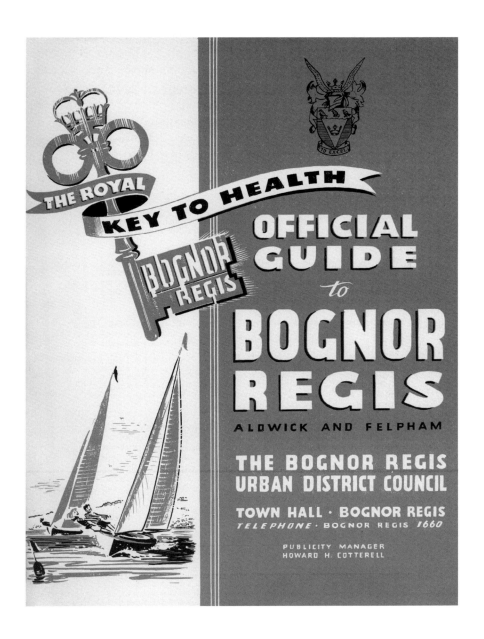

THE ROYAL **KEY TO HEALTH**

BOGNOR REGIS

OFFICIAL GUIDE *to*

BOGNOR REGIS

ALDWICK AND FELPHAM

THE BOGNOR REGIS URBAN DISTRICT COUNCIL

TOWN HALL · BOGNOR REGIS
TELEPHONE · BOGNOR REGIS *1660*

PUBLICITY MANAGER
HOWARD H. COTTERELL

that we return to the cottages for lunch and a rest before returning to the beach or more likely a drive in the countryside, which she preferred.

For special occasions, there were ice creams on offer at the Marine Café and the odd, very English lunch at the Green Lounge in Aldwick Road, which I recall was a very 1950s menu of soup, meat and two vegetables, and ice cream or cabinet pudding.

The pier was about slot machines and didn't excite me, but Bognor in the immediate post-war period had various backyard poultry-keepers and I was fascinated by them, particularly a large flock of chickens in Wood Street and geese behind Valetta Cottage. Grants, the greengrocers in Nyewood Lane, stocked fantastic summer fruit and strawberries and cream were a regular, totally seasonal treat. Prawns could be acquired from contacts of the Grays and cream teas were on offer in a garden in Bosham, which to my delight hosted an aviary of budgies.

It was simple stuff but Bognor Regis was crowded with young families in the 1950s, forming a moving crocodile to the beach. Those without beach huts went regardless of weather, emerging from a host of guest houses, small hotels and lodgings, dragging buckets and spades behind them. I felt proud that we had a cottage with the freedom of a small garden full of roses, honeysuckle and wild strawberries. To me, a London boy, Bognor Regis was not just seaside in the 1950s it was a country town.

David Allam
1st Chairman of the Bognor Regis Local History Society
High Sheriff of East Sussex, 2013

The Season

Bognor Regis – the holiday resort – was always absolutely full during 'The Season', which usually stretched from just after Whitsun until the end of the summer school holidays.

The 1950s followed the war and I remember summer after summer, that the part of the beautiful sandy beach between the end of Gloucester road and the end of Nyewood Lane, was absolutely packed with happy holidaymakers – in fact when the tide was coming in it was difficult to find a place on the beach to place a deckchair. The most popular part was between The Rex Entertainment Centre and the Royal Norfolk Hotel. On the corner of York Road, opposite the Rex, there was a wonderful toy shop called Goodacres that sold all the wonderful toys imaginable and also, of course, all the paraphernalia necessary to enjoy the seaside: buckets and spades, beach balls, kites, and bathing costumes and footwear for paddling in the sea.

Next to the toy shop was the Florida restaurant, a delightful seaside restaurant with a glass-covered canopy beneath which one could dine in all weathers. This restaurant was owned by the Kalli brothers who also ran the amusement arcade on the pier. Their sister ran the ice-cream stall next to the restaurant. She quite fascinated me because, where she was in the sun all day with her sunglasses on, she got very brown apart from her sunglasses-covered eyes. She looked like a panda. She was very beautiful.

By the ice-cream kiosk was the first set of amusements: ghost train, roundabouts, bingo stalls. This set of amusements was run by the Romain family. The Romain twins, Pauline and Johnny, were wonderful 'show people' who performed amazing jitterbug sessions at the Rex Ballroom that had all the other dancers spellbound (dances were held every night during the summer, apart from Sunday of course). Although in those heady 1950s the sun appeared to be shining continually, Johnny told me that he preferred a bit of rain because then the holidaymakers would come up off the beach to shelter and spend their money in the amusement arcades. I worked in the amusement arcade on the pier occasionally, when I was on leave from the Navy, so I knew that this was true – there was no custom on the Greyhound Racing at all when the sun was shining!

Next to the amusement arcade was the zoo with its imitation rock-faced cliff on which monkeys would clamber. It was from this zoo that a lion was said to have escaped in the 1930s when the news was broadcast nationally that the lion had been seen in Pagham. It all turned out to be a publicity stunt arranged, I believe, by Billy Butlin, the owner of the site.

Going west from the zoo there were sunken gardens with a small café, and several hotels including the famous Shoreline, which later became very popular as a club for young people where they could go and let their hair down.

Opposite the pier was a bowling green at Waterloo Square and a small crazy golf course, which was a favourite with elderly holidaymakers. This area and the pier itself were extremely popular. The pier had two theatres and an amusement arcade and there was also a very good café that was managed by my wife Pat. A train ran along the pier to the end where there was a small dance hall and diving boards from where divers – hooded, shackled and sometimes on bikes – would amaze large audiences as they plunged into the sea. There was a jetty at the very end of the pier from which paddle steamers, loaded with passengers, would sail down the Channel. The pier was a great centre of fun, on the top, at the end and even underneath.

Leaving the pier and travelling westwards, this part of the beach was the most popular for organised games on the sands, competitions, keep fit, small car races, Punch and Judy, and beauty competitions. The lower promenade had long rows of concrete steps leading down to the sands. These made an ideal 'grandstand' for watching the games and Punch and Judy.

I Do Love the Views at   BOGNOR REGIS   MABEL LUCIE ATTWELL

At this upper level of the promenade, opposite the Royal Norfolk Hotel, the delightful Esplanade Theatre was situated. Each summer the same show *Dazzle* was performed and the show became very much part of the summer scene of Bognor Regis. The cast made many friends locally and some of them eventually settled in the town.

Adjoining the theatre was a proper seaside café, run by Mr Macari, where one could get a welcome cup of tea and snack. Teas were often delivered on a tray down to the sands – this happened at several of the cafés along the seafront.

There were floodlights fitted next to the café which shone onto a large raft situated a few yards out to sea when the tide was in. At night the area was lit up, and on a warm summer's evening midnight bathing took place; with the dance music drifting across the water from the dance hall at the end of the pier, what a wonderful, romantic time it was.

I've tried to convey what an exciting and joyous place Bognor was in the summer. Visitors streaming from the train station to one of the 123 hotels and guest houses advertised in the local guide, a look on their faces of happy anticipation, a fulfilled anticipation that brought those visitors back to Bognor year after year.

It was also good for the residents I can assure you, we enjoyed it too.

Besides the amusements on the seafront there were other entertainments. The carnival, the local hospital fete, the large travelling fair that visited the town every August, and the show that was held on the Hampshire Avenue recreation ground each year. This show included a wooden house that was built, being set alight and the fire brigade racing up to save a screaming women (fireman dressed up). One year the fire brigade didn't arrive in time, and the house was completely burnt down by the time it got there. The poor 'lady' was quite alright though, having jumped from the top window well before.

Ken Scutt
Town Mayor 1995/6
Bognor Regis

TRAVEL

At the beginning of the 1950s many people were starting to take an annual holiday, mainly by the seaside, and Bognor Regis was a very popular destination. It is interesting to note that it was not until 1956 that the third-class rail fares ended.

Having studied the local newspapers of the 1950s we have found fascinating travel statistics recorded each year, including the monies collected for parking, entry fees and deckchair rentals.

In the *Advertiser* on Thursday, 20 August 1953, there is a story about the entire Pollard's Hill Tenant's Association travelling to Bognor Regis for the day, with special trains taking 600 people.

Bletchley excursion train, 30 June 1952.

British railway ticket.

The report continues:

POLLARD HILLS ANNUAL OUTING

One of the largest annual outings organised in East Surrey is that of the Pollard's Hill Estate Tenant's Association. On Sunday morning the Mitcham housing estate became almost deserted as 600 people left their homes and walked across Mitcham Common to Beddington Lane Halt, where they boarded a special twelve coach train and set off for Bognor Regis.

Everything had been planned with military precision. The 600 walked across the Common in parties of fifty, and were seen across the busy Croydon Road by a police patrol.

During the one and a half hour journey to Bognor Regis every one of the 363 children in the party was given a shilling [5p]. The shillings were carried to the train in a mysterious black bag by Mr W. Stephens, the Association's Treasurer. They had been supplied by an obliging gas company. A total of 3,500 half price amusement tickets were also given to the children.

At Bognor Regis a tent was erected on the beach as a headquarters and over it flew a P.H.E.T.A. flag. Throughout the day, two nurses from the Mitcham Red Cross detachment were on duty to treat minor casualties among the Mitcham party.

Everyone had forgotten that the tide would come in, and the tent was saved at the last moment as the waves lapped up to the guy ropes just after lunch. Eventually the headquarters party was squeezed off the beach on to the promenade.

Twenty two officials, including the association's president and chairman Mr T. Fitzgibbons and Mr T. Shanley spent part of their day on duty looking after the party.

The people of Pollard's Hill occupied a long stretch of the Bognor Regis seafront, and before long the braver ones were occupying the sea. The remainder preferred sand castles and donkey rides or deckchairs and newspapers, according to their age groups.

After they had spent eight hours in the resort, the Mitcham Party left Bognor Regis at 6.28 p.m.

'A really successful outing,' commented Mr Fitzgibbons as the people left the train at Beddington Lane Halt. 'It certainly was' echoed Mr Shanley.

The August bank holiday in 1950 saw more than 20,000 people arrive in Bognor Regis by train alone.

Day Trippers

Looking through the newspapers of the 1950s, it is interesting to see how various advertisements and articles were produced to encourage people to come to the town.

In January 1958, *The Scotsman* newspaper reported that, for whatever reason, over 11 million Britons never went away for a holiday. They continued the report by saying 'that one English seaside resort, Bognor Regis, was going to tackle the problem.' The Bognor Hotel and Restaurant Association were to provide out of season holidays at a fixed all-inclusive price of £6 guineas (£6.30).

When talking of their holidays in the 1950s, people's memories vary considerably due to where they lived, and their financial situation in relation to the methods of transport available. We must remember that war had only finished in 1945 and many forms of rationing continued into the 1950s. Items that were considered luxuries in the 1930s soon became available for more of the community. Sometimes it is quite difficult to imagine the 1950s as still being a time of austerity.

In the 1940s there were just over 2 million cars in the country and 'going out for a drive' was not really practical due to factors like the lack of petrol and smaller roads. However, in 1950 Vauxhall cars, rather than tanks*, began to be built, but with a shortage of steel this was not as easy as was first envisaged. By 1955 car ownership had increased, but only to 3.5 million. It was not until 1958 that the country's first motorway was opened, thus enabling the motorist faster access to places of interest, but still the price of new cars continued to be prohibitive to many people.

*Authors' Note – during the Second World War, the making of cars was changed to the production of 5,600 Churchill tanks.

Strolling along the prom on a cold day.

Day trippers enjoying a rest.

Buses and Coaches

The picture of a Southdown bus leaving the bus station was the No. 50 to Pagham. It was the part of the route from Middleton-on-Sea all the way through Bognor Regis via Felpham, Upper Bognor Road, turning left at the level crossing,

Leaving the bus station in the High Street.

Colin Bell, a bus conductor in 1954, during his summer vacation.

London Road, Spencer Street, Lyon Street and down the High Street to the Bus Station. It went through Aldwick, Rose Green, up around Hook Lane and down to Pagham where the terminus was, before you went into the shingle roads to the old railway carriages for holiday homes.

I became fascinated with buses which I spent a lot of time using. One such bus route, the No. 55, went to the bottom of Barrack Lane and turned at the entrance of a house owned by two elderly ladies who provided a kiosk for passengers and visitors to the beach. Double-deckers were utilised on the route in peak summer, with a conductor of course, but they were built for low bridges with a sunken gangway along the off side. This was because of the low trees at the approach to the terminus from

Southdown bus timetable 1955.

the entrance to Craigweil Estate, past the parade of shops which had a garage in it selling petrol at 4/9d (or 24p per gallon in today's money).

Clifford Jones
Sowerby Bridge, West Yorkshire

From the Back Garden

Looking back, summer evenings are remembered as warm and sunny. When it was too late to be allowed out and too early to be sent to bed, my brothers and I needed some occupation. It became a habit to sit on the wall at the bottom of our long garden at the end of Highfield Terrace, which then had the original name of St John's Terrace. We would watch the steady stream of coaches passing along Gordon Avenue on their journey home.

If there was short gap in the coaches we knew it was probably because the policeman, a special duty for the coaches, had halted them at the junction of

Gordon Avenue and Chichester Road to let the local traffic through. A larger gap indicated that the level crossing gates had been closed and on busy evenings, particularly at weekends, we knew that the coaches would be backed up along the Upper Bognor Road to what we called 'the Triangle' because the coaches had only just made the turn into Gordon Avenue, a residential and not very wide road, but in those days the residents did not have the number of cars that are parked there in 2014. They were going slowly enough for us to read where they had come from. As we waved to the passengers we called out the place names, not always knowing how they were pronounced. Back indoors, if time and inclination permitted, we were encouraged to get a map out and locate where the coaches had come from. Our family didn't travel much in those days so we were fascinated by place names such as Golders Green, Shooters Hill and Virginia Water.

Barbara Eldridge
Bognor Regis

It was interesting to learn that when the coaches parked in the coach park, a man called Tubby Isaacs arrived as well. He was well known in East London, for his eels and pie business, mainly selling outside pubs on a Sunday. He set up his jellied eel stand in the coach park to enable the passengers from London to buy his wares before they went down to the beach.

A packed East Coach Park, showing in the background the cranes used for the Esplanade extension to Felpham.

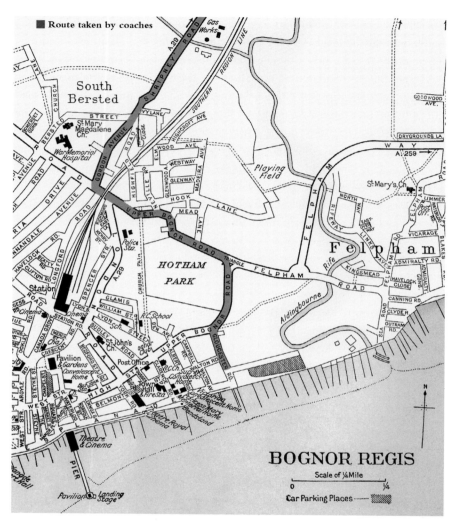

A 1954 Ward Lock's map showing the coach route out of the town.

On the Bypass

When I lived in Surrey, around 1952/3, I would cycle to see my friends in Dorking. On my return on a Sunday evening it was usual to see crowds of people lining the main A24 between there and North Holmwood, where I lived. These crowds would be sitting there waiting in anticipation of the drive past of sometimes over 200 coaches that had been to the seaside for the day. They were eagerly awaited – I suppose we thought of where they had been or were envious of their journey. It was not usual to see coaches and certainly not in the Sunday evening quantity.

Ann Manville, *née* Owen-Buerk
Bognor Regis

Sunday School Outing

As a young child in the 1950s I moved to Lewes from Manchester which was the start of a very different life. One summer I went on a day's Sunday school outing with my local church, accompanied by my father who was the local rector. We travelled by coach which unfortunately caused me to be ill. As soon as we arrived in Bognor Regis I remember being taken to Marks & Spencer, where a new set of clothes was purchased. It was the one and only time in my life that my father bought me any new clothes!

I then went on to have a lovely day running on the golden sands, splashing in the sea, eating a picnic on the beach, and, yet even more treats, my first donkey ride and an ice cream.

Anne Jeffery
Bognor Regis – U3A

The 1957 town guide.

A postcard view of cars parked along the Esplanade.

Cars

It is interesting to note the effect that the increase in motor cars had on the town, as can be seen from the following newspaper articles.

The *Bognor Regis Observer* from 3 June 1950 had the main headline, '37,000 Whitsun visitors – Endless stream of cars to Bognor Regis'. 'Nobody has ever known traffic like it here' commented a garage on the main London–Bognor road after a Whitsun weekend which, in the view of another garage proprietor in Bognor Regis, was far busier than any that had been seen since long before the war.

The owner of a garage on the Chichester Road declared that it was 'just like a race track' with a continual stream of cars passing, and concluded that 'it was evident that everybody who had a car was giving it an airing last weekend.'

No sooner had the car become a means of transport into the town then other reports were to reach the headlines. One such was *The People* on 23 December 1953, who reported that:

It costs a bob [5p] to park a car on the seafront at Bognor Regis – if motorists are foolish or generous enough to pay. For payment cannot be legally enforced; the seafront is a public highway. That doesn't prevent attendants asking for a shilling. Now the AA is advising drivers to keep their bob. A tip – yes, but not the automatic forking out of a shilling [5p]. Bognor Regis it seems is the only seaside resort with this system. Motorists get a ticket headed 'Bognor Regis Urban District Council – authorised parking places.' Beneath in small type is printed – 'While no charge can legally be enforced, attendants are authorised to ask for a contribution of a shilling towards wages!' Yesterday a council official said – 'If we didn't have attendants there would be chaos. Most drivers pay willingly. We make little out of it after paying wages.' Other seaside resorts in Sussex do not have attendants or charges.

The Aldwick Hundred Motor Cycle Club

The Aldwick Hundred Motor Cycle Club was founded in 1953 by a group of enthusiasts who lived mainly in Bognor Regis or who worked in and around the area. Motorcycling had become popular again after the war period, with new models being produced and prices coming within the reach of more people. The roads were far less congested than today and motorways in the UK were still in the future. With petrol at about 4s 6d (24p) a gallon, journeys to new places further away from home became a challenge with new experiences offered.

Weekends away were arranged at convenient times, with camping in the Forest of Dean being popular while some of the members got involved with more serious amateur sporting events in the South of England.

There were many social changes in the 1950s – not least the increase of family cars and the small new Mini (1959) seemed to point the way for things to come, providing more comfort in wet weather which seemed to set the seal on mass motorcycling. Perhaps the inevitable came about with the club folding after about eight or so memorable years.

Roy Laing
Fishbourne, West Sussex

ACCOMMODATION

Only a small percentage of people who gave us their memories spoke of or even remembered their accommodation, presumably because in the 1950s many of our contributors were about 5–12 years of age and the accommodation was not high on their agenda of holiday memories.

It was good to receive the memories of the visitors to the town, but it was also very interesting to hear from family members of those providing the service to our visitors. One such came from Australia:

Jean (left) and Margaret outside their parents' bed and breakfast at No. 45 Canada Grove.

My Home Bed And Breakfast

Due to my father's ill health, our family – Mum, Dad, my younger sister aged 6 and myself at 11 years old – moved to Bognor Regis in 1953 where my parents purchased No. 45 Canada Grove and opened up a guest house. I am Jean Shearley, *née* Mallindine, and with my husband and four children we emigrated to Australia in 1968.

Life at No. 45 was interesting and extremely hard work. We had six bedrooms and at times as many as twenty-six guests and for the first few years it was 'full board'. No sooner had one meal finished than it was time to start again. My mother did all the cooking with my help doing vegetables, cleaning, errands and waiting tables. As well, there were mountains of washing up and no dishwashers then!

The six dining tables had white damask tablecloths and napkins which were all changed daily. At first, Bognor Steam Laundry did the washing and it was all returned beautifully ironed and packed into boxes. However, my father thought this was too expensive and bought a huge washing machine which meant a lot more work, of course.

In the season my day started by going to Acres the Bakers for a huge bag of hot bread rolls. I can still smell them. Then I went home to make all the butter curls which was a tiresome job, with the butter either too soft or too hard. Then grapefruits had to be segmented and put into individual glass dishes. The tables had been laid the night before and I carried the hot breakfasts in on huge wooden trays. Thinking about it now, it's not surprising our guests returned year after year with this service and food; my mother was a wonderful cook.

Our guests became friends and I loved the children. Sometimes I would relieve the parents and take the children down to Butlin's amusements where they enjoyed playing on the slot machines and bumper cars.

We all dreaded 'changeover Saturdays' which meant all rooms had to be spring-cleaned, beds stripped and most times changed around to suit different-sized families. This meant my sister and I would struggle with mattresses up and down flights of stairs and we would end in hysterics which didn't please Mum!

My mother had a contract with Coventry Council and each September, the end of season, two foster families arrived to stay. There were thirteen children in each family, parents and a carer, which meant twenty-six children. We loved this time as it was great fun and my sister and I would take them out crocodile style down to the seafront. Although all were orphans, they were very happy children and really enjoyed their holidays in Bognor Regis, which would have been a real contrast to Coventry after the war.

When Butlin's Holiday Camp was being built we had several Irish labourers stay; they were quite interesting characters. Mum soon had them sorted out regarding hygiene and rules of our home! They had huge appetites too.

Winters out of season were very hard financially; we had a few travelling salesmen who stayed and odd people passing through. One couple woke us all in the night fighting and the husband was chasing his wife through all of the bedrooms, with a knife, ending up in our permanent guest's bedroom. A gentleman retired home from working in India, he was extremely shocked at all this happening at the bottom of his bed as he sat up with his nightcap on. My father managed to restrain the husband and sent the couple packing.

Number 45 was a beautiful house with double doors at the entry through to the paned front door complete with brass door knob. The room used as the dining room was large with a sashed bay window, deep skirting architraves and a rose in the ceiling. Each internal door had a crystal door knob and I often wonder what happened to those. My father was a very good handyman and kept it all in top condition. To furnish the house he used the furniture from our home in Essex and the rest was bought at Reynolds Auctions. My father used to strip all the pieces down and French polish them and although it was old fashioned most was good quality. I don't remember much laughter or fun in those days, but they must have been proud of their achievements. However, I think my mother was too generous to be a business woman and profits were low and in time our guests' children all grew up and stopped coming.

Jean Shearley, *née* Mallindine
Queensland, Australia

Teenage Memories

Having survived as a wartime child of the London Blitz, V2 rockets and a period as an evacuee, life was still pretty dreary for a 12 year old, with power cuts, massive snow drifts in the harsh winter of 1947 and bombed out buildings, but everything was about to change.

My mum and dad decided on a new life, by buying a guest house in Bognor Regis. They bought a lovely Edwardian house called Ravenscourt: it had eight bedrooms and a large lounge and dining room, both with double bay windows. In the winter time we had permanent paying guests from the end of September to the next Easter. They became friends of the family as they came back for many years well into the 50s. From Easter it was the holiday season, the cost per person ranged from £5 5s 0d (£5.25) in May to £7 17s 6d (£7.37) in August. Children sharing their parent's room with a nursery tea tray were half price. Meal times were early morning tea at 8 a.m., breakfast at 8.45 a.m., lunch at 1 p.m., and dinner at 6.30 p.m. Finally there were tea and biscuits at 10 p.m.

Around all this eating you had to pack in the beach and daily swim, visits to places like Hotham Park, Chichester, Pagham Harbour and Goodwood. There was no shortage of what to do after dinner, with a stroll along the prom, or plenty of entertainment with the summer show at the Esplanade Theatre – just across

RAVENSCOURT
Ellasdale Road,
Bognor Regis West

● Board Residence ● Garage ●

Highly recommended for quiet comfort, excellent cooking and service. Separate tables. Few minutes to Sea, 'Buses, Shops Putting Green and Marine Gardens.

TERMS: 5 to 7 Guineas (ALL INCLUSIVE)

No extras. Brochure from resident Proprietors : G. F. Nice . A. C. Cordiner Telephone 1939

A 1951 town guide advertisement.

The Ravenscroft Guest House in Ellasdale Road.

from the Royal Norfolk Hotel. There were also variety shows on the pier and three cinemas from which to choose.

To me it was like a perpetual holiday, having being deprived of holidays in the war years with no access to any beaches, because of the threat of invasion. I was now settled happily into Chichester High School, made new friends, was an early member of the Yacht Club, and spent my leisure time with St Johns Youth Club, sailing at the newly formed Bognor Regis Yacht Club, cycling up to Goodwood or Slindon Woods, especially at bluebell time. We also sampled the delights of the new innovation of a genuine Italian coffee bar, presided over by the genial Mr Macari. There was beginning to be pretty, colourful clothes in the shops for teenagers and no clothing coupons necessary! It was still a place of traditional family holidays before the 'package holiday' trade and yes, Bognor Regis was a good place to be, whether a visitor or resident.

Val Warlow, *née* Nice
Barry, South Wales – U3A

A Family Business

I was born in the mid-1950s in Millbrook Guest House, No. 92 Aldwick Road which was run by my grandmother Mrs D. Poole.

In my early days my family home was a guest house as my parents ran Richmond Lodge, No. 50 Richmond Avenue, whilst my auntie ran a guest house in Elm Grove.

As far as I can remember I was about 7 years old when I was given simple tasks I had to complete, and help my mother with her guests. My sister Rosemary was seven years older than me and from my being 10 years old I helped my sister to wash up and serve meals.

I consider I had a happy childhood although it was a hard existence as my mother was always working and couldn't take us down to the beach or shopping.

Mother could take thirty guests and we opened and closed the summer season with numerous 'over 60s' clubs. I remember them as a happy group of people, who, although they didn't go out much in the evenings, used our piano and spent the evening with a good sing-song. Sometimes out of season we would have children from a children's home for a period.

A thriving letting business kept so many people in work but it was very hard work for families.

The residents of Richmond Avenue were a close community and if we had a sudden excess of bookings, Mother would rent bedrooms from our neighbours,

The Gables Private Hotel
CRESCENT ROAD · BOGNOR REGIS

Ideally situated
close to Pier,
Shops, Railway
Station

Tennis Courts,
Car Park and
Gardens in front
of Hotel

Comfortable and pleasant bedrooms all fitted H. & C. water. Slumber-land beds and bedside lamps. Excellent food and cooking. Separate tables with efficient service. Comfortable lounge.

Terms: 5 to 7 Guineas. **Brochure on request.**
According to Season.

Telephone: Bognor Regis 1602. *Proprietors:* Mr. & Mrs. W. H. DACEY

A 1954 town guide advert.

just to sleep. They still ate at Richmond Lodge. By 1957, Mother had rented the whole upper floor from next door, so she had eight bedrooms to let.

We had two residents, retired professionals, who were almost permanent, staying with us on and off throughout the winter. Mainly our summer guests came from the South of England and London and stayed for one or two weeks and many returned most years. Saturday was changeover day when all of the bedding had to be changed for the new guests, quite a task.

Mother served three meals a day. These were set meals and there was only a small choice at breakfast. Most guests were on full board, only a small percentage were on half board. Each morning a jug of hot water was taken to the room for washing – also early morning tea. A typical breakfast was porridge/cornflakes, eggs and beans (commonly known as a 'cowboy breakfast') and toast. Lunch could be soup, liver/bacon, and rice pudding. The evening meal was something like soup, roast and ice cream.

As you must realise most of this was told to me by my mother when I was older as, although I talked to guests and played with other children, I didn't learn all these facts in those days.

Janet Rufey, *née* Hunt
Bognor Regis

Lyon Street Bed and Breakfast

I was married when I was just 19 in 1950, and my husband and I had a small house, but like so many we had to have a mortgage to purchase the home. We then arranged to let out at least one of our rooms in Lyon Street. It was an ideal spot as it was on the walk from the railway station to the beach and, of course, the return walks home to the station. At one time I had a gentleman who stayed for much of the summer, in one small box room. We let out another room for bed and breakfast. It was a double and could also take a single bed. There were many people letting out in Lyon Street, so I had a royal-blue piece of material, with orange writing stating that I had bed and breakfast. Many people would ask, 'Is your mother in?' as I was so young to be a landlady. People could ask for what they wanted for breakfast; for example, half a grapefruit, and smoked haddock was available. This would cost approx £2 guineas (£2.10) per week. They could sit in our lounge if the weather was bad. Some visitors would ask for a meal in the evening and this we did provide. Of course, some commodities were still rationed so we had to have the ration book if it was full board.

During the Goodwood Races we were constantly asked for accommodation and the men would say they would sleep in the bath, as any accommodation was very difficult to find in the area when the races were on. Some people would even sleep under the pier if they could not find anything more suitable.

The postcard message reads, 'This is where I have landed, all very nice and comfortable. We face the sea so it is very pleasant.'

One of our visitors had a stall on the seafront selling jewellery but only during the summer.

Sylvia Olliver
Town Mayor 1993/4, 1996/7, 2001/2 and 2004/5
Bognor Regis

From Bexleyheath

As a young child living in Bexleyheath, I spent a fortnight's holiday for three or more years running in Bognor Regis in the early 1950s. My late parents knew a Mrs Forbes and this is where we stayed in Highland Avenue. We travelled by coach or by train as my dad never had a car until 1955. I can remember the theatre and going there. In those days it was a treat to stay up later than normal bed time!

I was born in June 1944 and was brought up in Bexleyheath and my parents were originally from East London (West Ham) moving to Bexley just prior to the Second World War. I think Mrs Forbes was perhaps a widow (as no husband was around), and had been a pub landlady possibly in the East London area,

This 1958 view of the beach has the pier in the background.

as she was somehow known to my parents and/or possibly by my dad's older brother. She lived in a semi-detached house in Highland Ave, Bognor Regis. I think from the back-room windows upstairs you could see a church or convent backing onto the garden as I seem to remember being told of nuns living there, unless this was to make me behave!*

It was a bog-standard semi. We ate our meals in the front room downstairs and the back room was where Mrs Forbes lived and possibly slept as there were three bedrooms upstairs (I shared my parent's room as I was young) and sometimes there were two or three other guests. No en suite in those days – not even a wash basin in the room, so we had to share the bathroom facilities. I think from later conversations with my parents, Mrs Forbes had moved to Sussex and the house was rented. She probably ran the boarding house as a way of earning a living in the summer by taking people she knew and as there was absolutely no signage outside about it being a guest house, it may not have been with the landlord's permission!

We used to have full board which meant a walk to the beach or town in the morning and back to the lodgings for lunch and then back out again in the afternoon. My mother also later told me that in the early 1950s – not long after the end of the war, of course, although I was unaware at the time of that – it was easier to have all meals in the digs as in those days there were not all the fast food outlets we have now and there were still shortages in the shops and also there was little tolerance of children in restaurants.

Colin Manning
Roydon, Nr King's Lynn

*Authors' Note – it was a convent chapel.

London Evening Standard, 13 April 1954:
Week by the sea for old folk. More than 1,000 old age pensioners are going to Bognor Regis for a spring time holiday at reduced rates. They will pay £3 7s 6d [£3.37] for a week's full board. They would get the same food and attention as at peak season. There will also be free games of bowls, special cinema prices, free deckchairs, a free variety show and reduced taxi fares. Said Mr E.H. Russell, Chairman of the Hoteliers, Old Pensions Committee, 'the old folks are some of the finest guests I ever had in my hotel – everything is done for them. But some of the old ladies are so appreciative that they quietly make their own beds.'

Bedroom to Let

I was born in 1952 so was only 8 when the 1950s ended.

My mother grew up in Hawthorn Road and every summer her parents used to let one room to visitors so we as children had to budge up to free up a bedroom. This was in order to add to their meagre income, and I was told it was very common – most of their neighbours did the same. I remember them putting up a 14-year-old distant relative from London one summer in about 1959 and being surprised at her excitement at seeing the sea and I swear that she screamed as we came out of Hotham Park into the High Street then turned left towards the beach. It was such a normal sight for me but she'd never seen it before! I had to show her where the beach was, took her to Hotham Park, where she bought me an ice lolly from the café there, and showed her where the main shopping street was.

I remember Bognor Regis having three cinemas. I saw *Bambi* at the Picturedrome when I was aged about 4 – I don't remember ever going to the Odeon but I do remember seeing a film at the Theatre Royal and a play at the Esplanade Theatre.

I remember that as you got nearer to the beach, you could smell not just the salt air, which you still just about can above the smell of traffic fumes, but also winkles and crabs and I used to love the raised walkway down the left side of York Road on the way to the seafront. I remember the old bus station in the High Street with the two staircases going up in opposite directions and finding it funny that whichever one you went up, you ended up in the same place! Just snatches of things really, as is the way when remembering childhood things.

Angela Ford
London

Ration Books Handed In

We lived at Westcott, near Dorking in Surrey, and it was easy to get to Bognor Regis down the A29. It was also on the same railway line direct from Dorking North to Bognor Station.

We came for holidays and stayed at a boarding house in Gloucester Road. It was chosen as being near the sea, and the regime was very standard: breakfast at 8.30 a.m., lunch (the main meal of the day) at 1 p.m. and a high tea at 6.30 p.m. So you were continually going to and fro to the sea.

In front of the Rock Gardens we can clearly see both the upper and lower prom.

When you arrived you had to hand in your ration books for the week. Your ration of butter, jam, sugar, etc. was put on your table, and that was that. No coming back for seconds.

There was no choice of meals. You ate what you were given. Although one morning when smoked haddock was served for breakfast, my sister (aged 12 years) was given a scrambled egg. When my parents asked her why, she said she had smelt the fish and had gone down to the kitchen to tell the landlady that she would not eat it! My mother was not pleased with her.

There were no en suite facilities then. You had to share the one bathroom with all of the other boarders, so in the morning you had to keep a sharp look out for when the bathroom was free. I think baths were an extra cost and had to be taken at night. You also had to bring your own soap as that was on ration too and provide your own towels.

You were expected to be out of the boarding house all day when not having meals, so come rain or shine we had to get ready to go soon after each meal. We spent most of our time on the beach during the day. When it rained we went to the shops or had a walk around the amusements on the front, although we were only allowed to spend our pocket money on slot machines, etc., during the evening walk, otherwise it would not have lasted the week.

Lyn Baily
Arun West – U3A
Middleton-on-Sea, Bognor Regis

To The Seaside to Recuperate

When I was a child my grandparents would take me to Bognor Regis whenever I had been ill or for my summer holidays. I was ill most winters and later this was diagnosed as TB! After spending two or three months in bed I would be wrapped

BEAULIEU
PRIVATE HOTEL
ESPLANADE, BOGNOR REGIS

Resident Proprietor : Mrs. H. L. CHARGE.   *Telephone :* Bognor Regis 136

IMMEDIATELY FACING SEA, WITH PRIVATE GARDEN & VERANDAS

Central for Amusements, Town and Bowling Greens.   All Bedrooms
have Hot and Cold Running Water.   Central Heating or Gas Fires.
Public Rooms overlook the Sea.

Highly recommended for cuisine and personal attention.

Open throughout the year.   Special Terms for Winter.
Garage space available.

A FAMILY BUSINESS, ESTABLISHED OVER 25 YEARS.

One of the advertisements in the 1950s town guide.

up in a blanket and put in the back of my grandfather's car. I knew we were nearly at 'Boggor' (as I used to call Bognor Regis) when we went round the war memorial at Eastergate. I still love to see the lion's tail and when I was a child I would squeal, 'We are nearly there!'

We stayed at Beaulieu which was a hotel on the seafront. My grandparents would have a bedroom with a balcony and I would be on the floor above. The hotel had some permanent residents and there was one lady who was quite crippled. She would always sit in front of the television in the lounge. She had a large knitting bag and I would carry it for her into the dining room and then take it back to her chair in the lounge after the meal. She would give me sixpence (2.5p). One day I found someone sitting in her seat so I evicted them and was given an extra sixpence. My sixpences were spent on the tractor train which used to travel along the front.

In the dining room there used to be lady and gentleman portions. There was a very subdued honeymoon couple staying in the hotel and I remember my grandparents laughing (quietly) when across the dining room the waiter shouted, 'One gentleman lamb and one cold lady.'

My grandparents would hire a beach hut when it was sunny and we would go swimming. If it was a windy day we would spend it in the Marine Gardens, which are nicely sheltered. The gardens are the same as they were then and when I walk through them it brings back many happy memories of my playing with other children while my grandparents would sit and read the newspaper. Occasionally we would have an ice cream bought at the kiosk.

Whenever the races were on at Goodwood or Fontwell we would go and once or twice we went riding. I think the riding school was on the edge of the town. We would often listen to the bands playing and, of course, I built sandcastles most days.

Bognor Regis always did me good and I would go home with lots of energy and roses in my cheeks. One year Beaulieu had succumbed to floods and it was closed so we went to Bournemouth – it was not as good. However, in 1960 Butlin's came and my grandparents decided that Bognor Regis would never be the same so we stopped going. Fortunately my TB had burnt out and I didn't have to think I will be better when I get to 'Boggor'.

Fiona Huntley
Pagham, Bognor Regis – U3A

A House Rent

I can remember when I was 17 in 1953 our family came down to Bognor Regis and we rented a house in Nelson Road for a fortnight. I suppose this was at a time when not everyone came for a fortnight and many people used the bed and breakfast premises. My father and mother only rented a house for one year, after that it was a hotel. My mother felt she did not have much of a holiday.

I can remember we used to go to the Belle Vue Restaurant for some of our meals to save my mother doing the cooking.

Margaret Bryant
Bognor Regis

Caravans

One of the main features of this area was the number of caravans on the coast that were available for visitors. The press regularly mentioned these sites and in 1958 a council meeting was asked by an owner if they could increase the number of their caravans. This was rejected as there were already 5,000 in the town and the council felt this was sufficient. Some of the sites have long since gone, but some still survive in 2014. One such has been mentioned by visitors and that is the Riverside Caravan Centre which was started by Percy H. May with his son John, who had been invalided out of the Navy. They opened the site in 1954 and at that time there was only an ash road and a small number of caravans. Today there are approximately 650 on the site.

Just one of the many caravan sites in the area.

Caravan No. 6

My husband and I spent our honeymoon starting August bank holiday weekend 1957. We had difficulty finding our accommodation, having booked a caravan and taken possession of a key with a number '6' on it but we failed to take note of the address. We arrived in the evening and asked a policeman where 'the caravan site' was. He laughed and said something along the lines of, 'Which one? Take your pick.' We eventually found our site where there was a caravan No. 6 unoccupied and our key fitted the lock.

During our honeymoon we obtained Charlie Coon's autograph at a summer fair; he was my husband's piano-playing hero. There was a big marquee near the seafront where we went to a show. I enjoyed the entertainment until the show host asked if there were any 'newlyweds' in the audience. I put up my hand, much to my husband's dismay, and we were invited down to the stage, to the tune, 'Hello young lovers'. Our embarrassment was mollified to a certain degree as we received a gift, which we still have.

Jill Chapman, *née* Soane
Farnborough – U3A

A 1950s postcard advertisement for the caravan park.

Peter's Holiday

In August 1958 I travelled by train with two old school chums from Dartford to Bognor Regis. From the station we walked to the Riverside Caravan Park. As I remember it, we enjoyed two weeks of glorious sunshine. Our days were spent walking to the beach every day, kicking a ball about or swimming in the sea. We would then walk back via a fish and chip shop located near an old iron footbridge over the railway line. The chip shop owners must have been ex-stage people as I remember the walls were lined with photos of theatrical people. We then spent every evening in the Riverside club playing darts and cards (for matchsticks) and making half a pint last all night (funds were very limited at the time as I was an apprentice).

Peter Burrell (left) with friends Ted and Peter Cox.

By 1959 I had met my girlfriend Diana whose parents had a caravan on the Riverside site, where again we enjoyed more holidays, travelling down first by scooter, then eventually by car. We married in 1963 and this year we celebrate our golden wedding, so we have very fond memories of Bognor Regis.

Peter Burrell
Aldwick, Bognor Regis

A Week in a Caravan

As a family we spent a week at the Riviera caravan site for two or three years when we were young. I think we were there when it was the Suez Crisis (1956) and one of my aunts and cousins also came. We visited Hotham Park which we found to be very pleasant; there was also a small theatre (Esplanade Theatre) near the front.

I also remember that there used to be a competition to see how far people could fly off the end of the pier and a Mr Needham from Dorking/Westcott entered this and had some contraption like 'wings'. I don't think anyone got very far and they all landed quickly into the sea. I am not sure where Mr Needham

One of many hotels in the town, this one situated in Stocker Road.

lived but he had a daughter who used to enter the fancy dress competitions in Westcott and usually won. I remember her having a Festival of Britain costume one year which I think was professionally made.

Carol Benstead, *née* Tickner

Epsom Downs

MEMORIES

Sometimes memories flow and it is not always sensible or possible to categorise or divide such contributions, therefore we have decided to include the following recollections in their entirety.

I Was a Bandsman

My National Service was spent in The Alamein Band of The Royal Tank Regiment, which for three seasons, 1950 to 1953, played for two months each year at Bognor Regis: on the promenade bandstand in the afternoons and in Hotham Park in the evenings.

Those summers seemed to have endless sunshine. If it rained there was a possibility that we might miss a performance. Sometimes we hoped for this to give us a chance to go to the cinema but in the years when I sang we only missed two performances, one of which was typically on August bank holiday Monday when it poured down all day and the poor trippers from London arrived in their special trains and then camped out in promenade shelters with their children until the trip trains returned at the end of the day.

I have happy memories of singing in Bognor Regis, which was enjoying a post-war holiday boom. It was before the package holiday left the English beaches somewhat depopulated. There were large crowds along the

Alan Binns in 1951, a 19-year-old vocalist and bandsman with the band of the Royal Tank Regiment.

promenade and in the park and trainloads of day trippers from London. There was a lovely feeling of post-war happiness that perhaps is not present today. I was 19 years old and singing in public was a thrill. It had its moments, for instance when the jets from Tangmere screamed low along the prom when I was half way through 'A Wand'ring Minstrel'!

Singing in the band saved me from being sent with the tank regiment to Korea. I didn't ask to be in the band, I was just picked out by the selection officer who must have been aware that the band needed a singer. I had never played or sung in front of such large crowds of people before and it was a new sensation to be billed as the star turn. It didn't please some of the regular instrumental performers because I took many of the pieces that were originally their solos.

Our bandmaster, Lieutenant Bill W. Lemon, used to sit at the rear of the deckchair area whilst we settled in our places and set up our stands. When all was ready he waited for the Sergeant Major to signal that he could make an entrance. One day he sent a message for me to come over to his seat. When I got there he said, 'Well, how do you think you are doing?' I was a bit lost for words and said I thought I was doing alright. He said, 'Do you know that when you sing in the afternoon all the workers in the town hall stop for their afternoon break and open the windows wide to hear your songs?' Apparently Lt Lemon thought that was a sign of success.

A typical family group enjoying the deckchairs on the beach.

The dear old ladies who were my most ardent fans have all left their knitting and their deckchairs long ago, and even the young girls who fluttered their eyelashes to the bandsmen will be in their 80s like me. Happy days!

Our Billet

We were billeted in different bed and breakfast accommodation around Bognor Regis. Three of us stayed in a boarding house in Merchant Street, run by Bert and Mrs Pearce, where we all shared a large bed. In those days no one thought it was improper. We had a few laughs there.

Three in a bed in Merchant Street had its moments. Ray Applin, our flute and piccolo player, was like his instruments – a tiny, slim guy. He smoked like a chimney and wouldn't get up in the mornings so we used to leave him in bed. One morning as we all lay in bed we noticed a hole in the plaster above us in the ceiling. As we watched a wasp dropped out of this hole and landed on the bed. Two of us were out of bed with speed and we called to Ray that there was a wasp in bed. He grunted and told us, in the vernacular, to go away. He rolled over and it stung him. He sat up as if electrocuted, his little pop-eyes nearly starting out of his head, and clapping his hand to the sting he said in broad Dorset, 'Downt urt!' It's a moment I still cherish after all those long years.

Charley White and Malcolm Souley, bandsman friends of Alan Binns, strolling opposite Goodacres toyshop.

We dined at Merchant Street for every meal. We rose in time for breakfast at 9 a.m. in the dining room and then smartened up our uniforms and wended our way down to the fire station, where a room had been set aside for us to store the instruments, and to use as a general base. The programmes for the afternoon and evening were already posted by the band sergeant, Major Alf Clayton. We sorted out our folders and then the time was our own. The fire station was adjacent to the promenade and we were provided with a driver and lorry to take the larger instruments and the music stands, etc. to the park and the promenade.

After our duties were completed we drifted down to the beaches and enjoyed the sunbathing and the swimming. I remember that you had to go a long way out sometimes to get more than knee deep.

I have little memory of the layout of the promenade. I know we went to a milk bar set between the promenade and the main shopping street. It was a bit expensive for us but the proprietor was an ex-artillery man and we called the place 'Gunners'. Although I was a churchgoer, I made no contact with Bognor Methodists as the timetable didn't allow it. We did a six-week season but in my second year we did eight weeks.

Bandstand

The bandmaster thought my name Binns was not romantic enough. He thought Binns did not have an artistic ring to it, so he proposed to amend my first name to Allan and to replace my surname with my cherished middle name, Penrose, which came from my Cornish mother. My father was scandalised but in the end it didn't come about, probably because of military correctness. They had already bent the National Service Act by getting me to sing instead of driving a tank in Korea.

We were always working to a timetable. Only once in two years did I get to Chichester as I was scared to be AWOL at concert time. We worked seven days a week and played two concerts a day. I suppose for some of the musicians it was easy to sit there playing and hidden in the band, but I was on public view and my every action was monitored by the audiences.

My repertoire fades into the past but I remember the Gilbert and Sullivan songs 'Take a Pair of Sparkling Eyes' and 'A Wandering Minstrel'; 'The Flower Song' from Carmen, and most of the old-time Victorian Ballads that were still popular with the people of a certain age who attended the concerts.

Alan Binns
Burnley, Lancashire

The Seafront

I was born in Twyford Maternity Hospital in Sudley Road, Bognor Regis, in 1945 and was aged 5 to 15 during the 1950s. My parents moved to Middleton-on-Sea, Bognor Regis, after the war as they had been bombed out and thought it would be better here for my elder brother's asthma. They had visited before the war on holiday. My father commuted to London every day as did my brother later. But I never wanted to do that and have always lived and worked in this area. From ages 8 to 12, I went to Northcliffe School as a day boy, commuting by bus, and later bicycle, from Middleton. Also there at the same time was Michael Grade, later to become well known in the entertainment industry. The school buildings are still there in Upper Bognor Road, Spencer Terrace and are now converted to flats.

We built model boats and sailed them at Queen Elizabeth Boating Pool; it was always busy and popular. It is still there under the raised level car park near Argyle Circus at the top of Queensway. It had some plaques of different towns around the perimeter and you could sail your boat from one place to another. Some of those plaques were repositioned in the surface of the children's play area north of the sunken gardens and can still be seen.

The well-remembered boating pond, shaped like a map.

I remember a photographer with a monkey along the seafront, with whom you could have a picture taken. There were Punch and Judy shows in various places on the beach and there were also donkey rides available. I remember a red speedboat called, I think, *Miss Magic* – a very handsome boat it seemed to me then – which had a mobile jetty near the pier so that people could get on without wetting their feet.

Billy Butlin had amusements along the seafront – all sorts – ghost train, slot machines, etc. There was a toy shop called Goodacres on a corner of York Road which was a wonder to a small boy.

Hugh Coster
Felpham, Bognor Regis

One of Ron Whittington's speedboats.

Rafts and Boats

I grew up in Bognor Regis (I was 10 in 1953) and spent the greater part of summer days on the beach with my friends during the 1950s.

I remember the 'raft' very well, but I don't remember it being floodlit. In the 1950s there was no shingle on the part of the beach by the Esplanade Theatre and, as you know, there is a two-tiered promenade there, now buried. I remember the drop from the lower promenade to the beach was enough to allow us kids to dive into the sea from it at high water. Does anyone remember the '*Daily Mirror Holiday Raft*' (a publicity stunt by the national newspaper)? It was a fairly elaborate contraption with diving boards, slides, loungers and piped music, banners and pennants, like a huge floating four-poster bed. It was towed around the coast by a tug and anchored at holiday resorts for a few days. It visited Bognor Regis and was anchored a bit further out to sea from the raft, quite a swim in fact, made difficult by the strong east-west current. A lot of swimmers never made it and were picked up by a constantly patrolling motorboat as they were carried towards Selsey, much to our amusement.

My mother worked part-time in Goodacres, a treasure-trove, L-shaped shop with glass display counters and a separate model section with balsa wood in all sizes, glues and dope (a lacquer to finish the models.) Is this word still used in

A pontoon allowing visitors to climb aboard for sea trips.

this context? Another favourite spot was the groyne opposite York Road from where the motorboats plied: *Zip* and *Miss Magic* the speedboats and *Sea Hawk* and *Bounty* the larger motorboats. We were highly impressed to be told that *Sea Hawk* and *Bounty* had been at Dunkirk.

The pontoon or jetty for the boats was moved up and down the beach between high and low tides by a DUKW amphibious vehicle, much as the people moved up and down until at high tide when they were jammed on the shingle between the water and the prom, and hardly a square inch was to be had. At that time the shingle was 2–3m below prom level. Whole days were spent on the sands playing football, hand tennis and tip-and-run (if anyone remembered a cricket bat), but the highlight was high tide when you could walk into deep water off the shingle and (if you could get away with it) sneak onto the pontoon and have a quick dive, risking a thick ear from the operatives. What did we do all day? In all the years I never went on the boats, it was too expensive, about 2*s* (10p) for the speedboats, but the motorboats were less. We saw paddle steamers visit the pier and there was a diving display on it regularly.

I know things seem much bigger when you're young but I remember crowds of people at weekends. The prom was black with them and you had to dodge through the crowds to move about. Hundreds, if not thousands, played on the sands at low tide. I always had the impression that most day visitors came by train as they seemed to dissipate en masse, leaving us to collect the unreturned 'Tizer' bottles for the 2*d* bounty.

Len Norman
Bognor Regis

Caravanning

I can remember coming down with Mum and Dad from 1954. The first year we stayed at the Pinehurst Caravan Park in Rose Green and the second time with Mr Baldwin in Canada Grove, who also owned an electrical shop in London Road. We lived in Cheshunt in Herts. My dad for a time worked in Storrington and we came on holiday in his green Hillman Minx, EEV 21, which I eventually had when I was old enough to drive.

We would go to the paddling pool that was shaped like a map of England. We also went to the Pixie restaurant/café to get super fish and chips, but my major memory was going to Delmonico's in the arcade where we also had Kunzel cakes, which we loved.

Going shrimping. Jennifer (left) next to Gillian with cousins Joan and Peter and their parents.

On the beach we saw Punch and Judy, and sandcastles were being made, except under the wall where there were stones. We never really used the large Rex building on the prom as we enjoyed going on the rocks to look for shrimps and crabs. We did sometimes swim in the sea opposite the Macari's café by the Esplanade Theatre. Another memory I have is of going into an International Stores with green and cream tiles, where they used to cut the cheese with a wire.

Paul Rapley
Bognor Regis

Ice-cream parlours became very popular in the 1950s, as teenagers took to their relaxed atmosphere rather than the cafe's used by their parents. It wasn't long before you'd hear, 'Meet you in the I.C.P. at 6 p.m.' – shortening words to initials is not new! The two local parlours remembered the most are Morelli's and Macari's.

Grandma's Cottage

I used to come down to Bognor Regis in the school holidays and stay with my grandmother Minnie Harrison (*née* Cox). She lived at Granville Cottage, No. 3 Canada Grove, one of a pair of cottages that for years later were blighted by

Our gang having fun on the beach.

plans for a roundabout linking to Argyle Road, but are still standing. My room backed onto a dairy (now a car dealership) which was extremely noisy in the early mornings. Grandma's cottage had an outhouse in which stood the toilet and bathroom. The water was heated by an Ascot over the bath and there was no ventilation unless you opened the window – an absolute death trap. She had a mangle in the yard outside and a spinning wheel on the half landing up the stairs. I used to love playing with these. The cottage also had (and still has) a side passage which I was scared of.

I remember very well going almost next door to the Co-op grocers (next to the Masonic Hall). They had an overhead cash system. When you paid your money, it was put into a capsule which shot across the room to a counting house.

I also remember there was an archway opposite the cottage leading to the boating lake (shaped like England) where I sailed my clockwork and sailing boats. To the side of the arches were poster boards for the Bognor Regis Entertainments Department. One of them advertised Cyril Fletcher in *Summer Masquerade*, but I don't remember going to the Esplanade Theatre until the 1960s.

The beaches of course were really golden in those days and there were steps down. But I spent a lot of time playing the slot machines, especially on the pier. My grandmother occasionally took me to matinees in the Roof Garden theatre where a repertory company was in residence. The pier manager was Claude Flude and he had been there for years. She also took me to whist drives in a house at the end of Cavendish Road, where I was the youngest player by around fifty years!

I remember going to the seafront with my cousin and daring each other to jump the waves crashing over the Esplanade – we often got soaked.

Anthony Wills
London

In 1959, according to local historian Gerard Young, 'the late 1950s saw the birth of optimism for Bognor's future; a spirit largely fostered by a councillor whose high-flown phrases and glorious enthusiasm were a tonic – for a while!'

Sand and Beach Games

I was born and lived in Gloucestershire until I was 5 years old, before moving to Surrey in 1957. I have no recollection of any seaside visits until I went on the annual Sunday school outings from Purley Baptist Church to Bognor Regis in the late 1950s.

The return train journeys were themselves a great adventure. Although much about them has changed in the last fifty years, the Bognor Regis railway station itself remains a vivid reminder of my childhood, having been restored in the 1990s much in the style of the 1950s.

The afternoons on the beach were a new experience long before the days of more sophisticated theme parks and other visitor attractions. The simple pleasures of beach games, sea swimming and ice creams were considered a real treat when my friends and I neither knew nor craved anything greater. These were Saturday outings just before the school summer holidays and although there were plenty of other people on the beach too, I don't remember it being quite so crowded as some contemporary photographs portray – perhaps they were taken on bank holidays!

Relaxing.

Enjoying an ice cream.

My only negative memory is of finding sand from the beach in my packed lunch's cheese and cucumber finger rolls on the first of those outings. It made them inedible and me distressed, but was a sharp learning curve for future visits to any beach.

Peter Williams
Ardeonaig, Killin, Scotland

A Fortnight's Holiday

I think we holidayed in Bognor Regis probably three years running – maybe 1950–2. I hated the coach journey there and had to crunch a Kwell travel tablet with a sweet, as I could not swallow tablets. I seem to remember two coach trips there but also going by train one year which I loved. The coach trip involved dad and mum carrying the cases for a good 15 minutes' walk to the coach stop in Bexleyheath, then getting on a Timpson's 'feeder' coach (now National Express) to the coach station in Catford (long since closed) where you had to change coaches to whichever destination you were going.

On arrival in the Bognor Regis area I seem to remember looking for the LEC factory on our left and then we felt we had started our holiday. The coach used to stop near Hotham Park where we got out and made our way to Mrs Forbes. There was a Southdown single-decker service which fascinated me because its headboard read something along the lines of – Service 51 Clockwise and 51 Anticlockwise which I suppose meant it was a circular bus route of the town area.

In 1950, mothers were still putting neat olive oil on their children's skin when playing on the beach. Self-tanning lotion didn't come on the market until the early 1950s and was very popular with young men and women wanting a quick tan. The white look was definitely out!

One of the routes from the railway station to the beach.

We used to go on the beach most days if the weather and tide permitted – so, if in the morning it was high tide, we went on the beach in the afternoon and vice versa. In the evenings, if not going on the pier or to the Esplanade Theatre, we often walked along the seafront to the Aldwick end of the town. I still remember the Tamarisk trees in this location by the footpath next to the beach, and a pub next to this pathway where sometimes we went into the beer garden and I had an orange drink; in those days there was no Fanta or Coke, just orange cordial. Also, in Marine Park Gardens there were seats in shelters for wet or windy days very near the seafront. Some had seats on their roofs and in good weather we sat there with a delicious ice cream bought from a nearby ice-cream parlour.

There was also a model boating pond in gardens somewhere in the town area, and we spent many an hour sailing a model yacht in this pond which was man-made and not deep; my mother would sit and knit and my dad read the paper. As a treat they would buy grapes or other fresh fruit in season from a greengrocer roughly opposite a church in a main road in the town (in those days you tended to have fruit and vegetables in season, unlike today when anything is available anytime).

We always had a fortnight's stay there (Saturday to Saturday) and my parents said they believed Mrs Forbes remarried, if so maybe she moved or stopped taking guests, but we never went there again. In 1955, once we had the car, we abandoned the public transport and drove to Wales, the Lake District and Scotland for our holidays.

Colin Manning
Roydon, Nr King's Lynn

My Home Town

I remember I was 8 in 1950 and living with my parents and my brothers, Graham and Gordon, in Victoria Drive. My father was mayor twice between 1947 and 1950. He was manager of the gas and electric showrooms in Argyll Road, where Sutherland Court is now.

During the summer my family and I used to swim a lot from the beach at Aldwick. My mother wouldn't let us have swimming lessons so we used to swim as near as we could to the lady giving swimming lessons to other children and copy her. We used to have long walks on the prom and treats at Stanley's ice-cream parlour. We spent a lot of time in Marine Gardens – there was a parade inspector there who kept an eye on things. We had hoops to play with and a friend gave us her roller skates so my brother and I shared them.

Donkey rides on West Beach.

Along the seafront I remember Punch and Judy, penny arcades, a 'fantastic' pier with lots of shows, a cowboy who used to come with his horse and ride around Bognor Regis displaying his skills with a whip.

There were donkeys on the beach – there was more sand then and you had to jump down to the beach. There were pedalos, speedboats and because of the pier, boats like the Waverley came. I also remember watching Tarzan diving off the pier. We would go to the Esplanade Theatre to see all the operatic shows, and also the *Dazzle* shows.

There was a boating lake shaped like England, with named towns round the sides. My brother fell in once and had to go home dressed in girls' clothes, which is now a family joke. The boating lake was lovely and they just took it away and now it's there under the car park.

In the town next to Reynolds there was a really upmarket café with polished brass called Leslie's. There was Osborne's, the bakers café, and Turners at the top of Station Road. There were loads of ice-cream parlours – a big one where

The *Bognor Regis Post*, 22 September 1951:
'No longer will beach donkeys, Kit, Jack, Molly, Jane and Mary canter on the sands of Bognor Regis with their loads of happy holiday children.' They were purchased by the 'Our Dumb Friends League', from Mr Octavius Smith to be rested and passed on to other seaside resorts.

the Waverley is now – but I cannot remember any fish and chip shops so perhaps they came later. We got our fresh fish from the fishermen on the beach.

My father was a founder member of Bognor Regis Yacht Club so we used to go to parties there. It was also where I and my younger brother learnt to sail. We loved just to sit and watch everyone sailing.

There were loads of things to do in Hotham Park; there was a big tent with a clown who entertained us, a boating lake and Pets Corner with a lot of small farm-type animals. My father was a founder member of Hotham Park and donated a lot of rabbits and guinea pigs in cages.

As a teenager I looked after two young children in the summer and took them out – to the beach, to Hotham Park and to east Bognor Regis to watch the military bands and Scottish bands which used to play there.

The town was always busy then; it was unbelievable how many guest houses and hotels there were in Bognor Regis. There were far more day trippers and holidaymakers everywhere you looked.

Eileen Anderson
Town Mayor 2009/10, 2012/13
Bognor Regis – U3A

A Family Affair

We stayed at the Sandilands Private Hotel in Stocker Road and in 1952 it cost £19 14s 6d (£19.73) for the five of us for a week, plus an extra 2½d per day for early morning tea for Mum and Dad.

We travelled in 1952 from East Ham in London to Victoria Station to catch the Bognor Regis train which departed from Victoria at 9.18 a.m. arriving in just under two hours.

In 1952 my brother left his bucket and spade behind on the beach. The following year it had disappeared and he was so upset; he was consoled with a double ice cream and a new bucket and spade.

We children would spend the morning on the beach doing what every other child did in the 1950s and that was build endless sand castles with our metal spades with wooden handles and metal buckets. We would paddle and swim in the sea while our parents lazed in deckchairs, father in jacket and tie and mum in her summer dress.

On the seafront there was Harrison's Amusement where the Regis Centre now stands. It had greyhound racing where you rolled a ball up, it fell through a hole and off went your wooden greyhound, the higher the score hole the further it moved.

Kay with her brothers, Richard (left), James (Jim) and mother Yvonne near Marine Drive West.

The dodgems were always a favourite in the amusement arcade on the corner of York Road with Morelli's Ice-Cream Parlour opposite, where in later years I would purchase many a great ice cream not forgetting their famous Rum Baba. In 1958, I had my first holiday on my own and I spent most days on the beach and in the evenings headed for the seafront, to the bars enjoying my favourite tipple, a pint of Brown Ale. Today's fancy names did not exist. Then I went to the amusement arcades where all the teenage girls congregated.

Kay Fall
Pagham, Bognor Regis

Excerpts from 'Memories of Bognor Regis' by Richard Smith available in the Bognor Regis Museum. His wife Sheila assisted with some of our early research, but sadly died before publication but his sister Kay continues to assist.

Weather and Holidays

Les Allatt was 95 when he was interviewed by Helen Krarup in October 2012, but sadly died a few months later. We are grateful to his family for permission to use his words in this publication.

The Royal Hotel in 1954, one of the prominent hotels overlooking the beach and pier.

Les was 31 when he came to Bognor Regis in September 1948 for an interview with the Chief Public Health Inspector. He obtained a post working with the medical officer, so moved his family down here to Felpham. His wife worked in the food office and their two daughters were aged 5 years and 1 year.

In the summer they took the children on the sands at Felpham. He described it as being ideal for children and there were always lots of holidaymakers. Along the prom from Felpham, along to the pier, there was a deep drop of 5–6ft onto the concrete edge along the sands and no railings, so he used to be very concerned for the safety of the children who cycled along there.

He clearly remembered getting off the train, periodically, to see the town was 'teeming with people' coming off the sands back to the boarding houses and hotels. At one time, before he moved, he had great difficulty finding a bed and breakfast and ended up in an attic in Argyle Road for the night. During the 1950s the town had more than twenty hotels, plus many boarding houses and bed and breakfast places.

In 1954 he became the Bognor Regis Meteorological Officer, a post he held until 1978. Part of his job was to record all the weather temperatures at different levels from 4ft down to 4ft above the town. He collected in all the information

from the weather station which is now
sited on top of the Fitzleet building.
He told me they had a page in the
annual town guide setting out the
weather statistics over the last thirty
years and that Bognor Regis and
Worthing were usually the top two
sunshine towns.

Hotels at that time included the
Royal and just beyond the Esplanade
Theatre was a long hotel, The Royal
Norfolk, which had more bedrooms
than the Royal Hotel. Along the prom
section in Aldwick it was practically
all hotels and holiday accommodation.
The queen and some of the royal
family stayed in Arundel and on the
seafront at the Bay Estate. In the
1950s Princess Marina brought
the children to the Carlton Hotel.
Princess Alexandra was one of
her children.

Les and his wife used to go to
the Rex where they went to police
dances etc. He told me that the Chief
Medical Officer in Bognor Regis
at the time was Michael Ayres
(the school was named after
him then – now South Way School).
He had a Children's Care Fund and
a lady called Mrs Watson put on
a whist drive in the Rex Ballroom
which had 150 tables round the
ballroom. The Rex building used to
be busy with people having meals.

Where Butlin's car park is now, at
the bottom of Gloucester Road, there
used to be scores of coaches every
day, seven days a week in the summer,

Leonard Lee in 1954 with the last of the
Landau's giving holidaymakers a ride along
the seafront.

From a town guide in 1950 extolling the virtues
of this large venue on the seafront.

The *Bognor Regis Post*, 2 April 1954:
During a council meeting discussing the Butlin's site on the seafront, one of the councillors remarked, 'away with these sites in accordance with the development plan they say', and he adds that he thinks this 'would regulate the tripper trade with a view to recapturing the "family resort" atmosphere that old Bognor always encouraged.'

with day trippers coming from London mostly and also the Home Counties. The holiday brochure had 'Visit Bognor's Golden Sands' on the front. Adjacent to the coach park was a miniature railway.

Butlin's had amusement arcades on the seafront from the mid-1930s. There were donkeys on the beach every day and they were kept in a field in Felpham, where horses and ponies are now near the bypass. He could remember seeing them being led down when he was cycling to work. There was also a tiny sweet and cigarettes shop on the corner of Gloucester Road and the High Street.

There were three cinemas in the summer months and four in the winter. The biggest was the Odeon (now the Bingo Hall), the Theatre Royal (behind the Rex – a nice cinema with a balcony), the Picturedrome and one on the pier in

In the centre of the Esplanade we can see the amusements and bingo belonging to Billy Butlin and Johnny Romain.

the winter. The first time I went you could hear the waves underneath. It was a theatre in the summer and there was the Esplanade Theatre which held 700 people. It had a variety of artists of quite good standing.

Les Allatt
Meteorological Officer 1954–78
Bognor Regis

The Times, 19 April 1954:
'Thousands of holiday-makers who sought relaxation and recreation in rural surroundings and by the seaside yesterday enjoyed the early evidence of spring in fitful sunshine and in spite of chill winds. The heaviest traffic was on the London to Brighton … with Bognor Regis roads heavily congested.'

A Free and Happy Life

These recollections were told to Helen Krarup by Julie Scott.

For Julie Scott, Bognor Regis in the summer was a wonderful place; everyone was friendly and you felt very safe all the time. Again, later, she said, 'We just had this lovely, free, happy life.'

She found the Rex Ballroom a wonderful place. They used to go dancing there regularly, and young men from the RAF station at Tangmere would come over to the dance hall and they all had a brilliant time. No one ever had to go home alone because someone would always see them to their front doors and make sure they got there safely. She mentioned that in the summer months there would be coaches coming from Chichester with young people who would be arriving to attend the dances in the Rex Ballroom on the seafront. And there were the *Dazzle* shows where famous comedians would come to Bognor Regis.

She mentioned a milk bar, Macari's, and that Mr and Mrs Macari were a lovely young couple who used to greet them and come over to chat to them and never minded how long they sat there.

She added that a lot of the people who came down to Bognor Regis in the summer came from London and that, when it was Goodwood week in July, a lot of the visitors who were going there would come to Bognor Regis to stay at places like the Royal Norfolk, when the place would be packed.

Peter Tomkins eating ice cream with his friends in Macari's ice-cream parlour.

She was an apprenticed hairdresser to Andre, who had come to Bognor Regis from London, and therefore many of the Goodwood visitors knew him and came into the salon to have their hair done.

She remembered Craigweil Lane as just that – a lane, where they picked blackberries – and said they didn't go on the beach much as it still had barbed wire on it from the war. She said that when the beach was sandy, especially by the pier, the water used sometimes to come up as far as the High Street, so the rocks and shingle were brought and the Esplanade changed. She said it took several years to clear the wire.

She mentioned several times how important Goodwood was to the town and that a lot of people came down here and decided to stay. People came to Bognor Regis by train and brought a lot of money to the town – everything was geared up to take your money then.

At the top of Craigweil Lane was a house called Aldwick Hundred owned by Mr and Mrs W.D. Watson. They used to see all the old cars coming down there for a party after a particular 'run'. Later it became a children's home for underprivileged children and was called Martineau House.

Julie Scott, *née* Edwards
Bognor Regis

Sailing as well

These memories came from a talk with Maureen Lord, who was aged 8 in 1950 and lived in Aldwick Gardens.

Maureen (left) with cousins Monika and Zeta Twine.

Val Nice in 1952, crewing for Rosemary Downer (right) in the B.R.Y.C Regatta.

Maureen remembers the Macari's restaurant. Maureen and her parents would catch the 9.15 a.m. bus from Aldwick to go to church and then walk back along the seafront calling at Macari's on the way. When she was a teenager she and her friends would go into Macari's, order a coffee each, and then sit for hours chatting.

When Maureen was 13 she and her friend Barbara joined the Bognor Regis Yacht Club. Barbara's parents bought a Firefly (dinghy) for Barbara and her brother, but as he was at boarding school it was Maureen that Barbara sailed with. Her parents also joined and her mother met up with many people whom she had lost touch with. During the war many people lost touch with each other and it was only towards the late 1950s that they began to reconnect. Bognor Regis Yacht Club at that time was very active and had fleets of Merlin, Cadets, Graduates, Fireflies, Enterprises and held many open meetings for the different fleets. In 1959 the Bognor Barrel open meeting for Merlin Rockets was held and continued until the present day. Maureen spent many hours at the yacht club, cycling down every day to sail. She doesn't remember holidaymakers coming down to sail, but said that some weekenders came down regularly from the suburbs to sail, staying in holiday homes or caravans.

Maureen also told me of a raft that used to be moored on the seabed, near the café which Macari's used to run in the summer near the Esplanade Theatre, for people to dive and swim from.

Maureen also remembers a hotel called The Carlton which had a terrace. Her grandma lived in Wellington Road and her family would sit on the terrace and stroll along there on Saturdays and Maureen would have lemonade and crisps.

Maureen Lord, *née* Austin
Aldwick, Bognor Regis

ENTERTAINMENT

Part of the excitement of going on holiday is the anticipation of what we will find there. For children, a seaside holiday features mainly around the sea and the beach and all of the other attractions are an extra bonus.

When Sir Richard Hotham laid the first foundation stone of his resort on 18 January in 1787 it was for 'a Public Bathing Place at Bognor in the Parish of Berstead', and he was to have no idea how this new place would develop. He hoped for a second Brighton which would attract royalty and, although this did not occur, visitors did arrive and enjoy their stay as can be read in the following memories.

URBAN DISTRICT COUNCIL ATTRACTIONS

FAMILY FUNTIME—EASTERN ESPLANADE BANDSTAND

● **BANDSTAND . HOTHAM PARK**
ORCHESTRA — presenting Light Orchestral Music, Novelty, and Request Programmes.

● **SANDS—OPPOSITE ESPLANADE THEATRE**
ORGANISED P.T. :: SPORTS, GAMES AND COMPETITIONS.

● **WATERLOO SQUARE**
BOWLING GREENS . TENNIS COURTS . CRAZE-E-GOLF . GARDENS.

● **MARINE PARK GARDENS**
PUTTING GREENS.

● **SWANSEA PLACE TENNIS COURTS** (Hard and Grass); Entrance, WEST STREET or VICTORIA ROAD.

● **BANDSTAND — EASTERN ESPLANADE**
Leslie Press presents FAMILY FUNTIME; Punch and Judy; Magic and Ventriloquism; Talent Competitions. From 11th July.

● **HOTHAM PARK, PETS' CORNER** — ANIMALS . BIRDS . BOATING POOL . PUTTING GREENS and ILLUMINATIONS.

● **EAST COACH PARK** MINIATURE RAILWAY.

MUSIC IN THE PARK

FOR EASTER, WHITSUN, EARLY & LATE SEASON ATTRACTIONS AND FURTHER DETAILS OF THESE ENTERTAINMENTS, which are subject to alteration, WRITE ENTERTAINMENTS MANAGER, ESPLANADE THEATRE, BOGNOR REGIS.

Hotham Park

Following a century and a half of private ownership, wartime use and neglect, the public bathing place was formally transformed into 'Hotham Park' in May 1947, so that by the 1950s it was a favourite destination for everyone as word of mouth had spread the virtues of this slightly hidden area. In May 1950, Pets' Corner opened and soon became a major attraction and by 1955 had been visited by no fewer than 1,106,620 people. The remainder of this park, which for so long had been the private grounds to numerous notables in the town's history, was suddenly a playground for all age groups. For children it was possible to cycle around with the help of a 'professional starter'. Races were a regular event and just a short walk away it was possible to enjoy a trip on the ornamental lake in one of a number of small motorboats, while parents could sit around the edge of the pool.

The Scotsman, 9 January 1958:
'A remark in a London letter stated: Bognor, renowned for its air, sunshine, sands and background of Sussex Downs, is one of the few popular seaside resorts near London which has wisely retained its overgrown village character. It has no need to pretend to be a seaside London, though it can and does absorb the crowds.'

Younger children could wander through various exciting areas, including one which contained figures of nursery rhyme characters such as Humpty Dumpty and the old woman who lived in a shoe; even Miss Muffet with her spider could be explored.

The following recollections will extol more details of this much loved and popular park:

Pets' Corner

Judith and Malcolm Roberts, 1956, enjoying themselves in Hotham Park Pets' Corner.

The greatest thrill for me was Pets' Corner as I loved animals, and the boating lake. The various delights included mostly small domestic animals and a variety of stone ornaments representing nursery rhyme characters. When small enough my favourite was The Old Woman Who Lived in the Shoe, a shoe that I enjoyed sitting in. In Pets' Corner the pens were small and the most exotic animals on offer were llamas and small monkeys and I recall a very sad mynah bird alone in a cage near the exit. The park seemed to be filled by white doves and was very tranquil, romantic and large. It was, to me, magical.

David Allam

The *Bognor Regis Post*, 6 December 1958:
'Over 189,000 children and adults visited Pets' Corner in Hotham Park in the past season. The numbers using town car parks was 112,379.'

A DELIGHT FOR THE CHILDREN !

PETS CORNER

HOTHAM PARK

ANIMALS —— BIRDS
BOATING POOL —— TRICYCLE RIDES

Come and see **HUMPTY DUMPTY, THE OLD WOMAN WHO LIVED IN A SHOE, MISS MUFFETT'S SPIDER'S WEB—YES, and the SPIDER.**

*Admission:—***Adults 6d.   Children 3d.**
*Season Tickets:—*Children and Adults:—Monthly 2/6, Season 5/-.

The 1953 advertisement in a Coronation celebratory programme.

Evenings with the Band

Evenings in Hotham Park were similar to afternoon concerts at the bandstand on the Esplanade. 'A Brown Bird Singing' and 'Trumpeter, What Are You Sounding Now?' come to mind, and we always ended with 'Sussex by the Sea' – in which the whole band that were not blowing sang the refrains. Sunday nights were emotive. We always ended with 'Nightfall in Camp' that included 'The Last Post' and 'The Evening Hymn'. I often sang the wonderful 'Shadows of evening around us are softly falling' from *L'Arlessienne* by Bizet. It had a thrilling high climax 'Darkness ending! Light is descending' which still brings tears to my eyes when I hear it. When my chapel organist, who knows I am listening, plays it as a voluntary I am tempted to stand to salute, first to the left and then to the right and finally to the front as I did in the park.

Alan Binns

A relaxing afternoon listening to the music in Hotham Park.

The Esplanade Theatre

Charles Powell is now retired but he was entertainment manager for the Bognor Regis town council for many years, including the 1950s, and he shared his memories with Anne Barrow.

It was not until 1951 that the well-remembered theatre was completed, providing a racked auditorium with 720 seats.

Charles Powell kindly allowed us access to some of his records of the various acts who appeared at the very popular Esplanade Theatre. He was responsible for booking all the acts for the summer seasons and felt that much of the success of the theatre was due to the local amateur groups who used the premises.

It is interesting looking at the various shows and names that appeared as many went on to become famous TV stars. The *Dazzle* shows are mentioned frequently and appear for six seasons from 1952, recommencing in the 1960s. Clive Dunn became the resident comedian in 1953–4 with Dick Emery appearing in 1955. Other new stars included Petula Clark in 1958. Over the years there were many special shows or summer shows, and appearing in these were numerous new names such as Johnny Dankworth and his then singer Cleo Laine, Acker Bilk, Edmund Hockeridge and so many others.

WEDNESDAY to SATURDAY: 3rd to 6th MAY, 1953
BOGNOR REGIS OPERATIC SOCIETY *present* **"YEOMAN OF THE GUARD"**
See Posters for times and prices.

Sunday, 14th May, at 8 p.m., FENNA OPERA CONCERTS *present*
A Full Concert rendering in English of the delightful Viennese Opera
DIE FLEDERMAUS

SATURDAY, 20th JUNE—FOR THE SEASON. RETURN OF YOUR POPULAR
SUMMER SHOW ! **"DAZZLE"**
WITH ERIC ROSS and IDA WILLIAMS and OLD and NEW FAVOURITES
NIGHTLY at 8 p.m. MATINEES Wednesday at 3 p.m. Constant change of Programme

A 1953 advertisement for the very popular Esplanade Theatre.

The Old Bailey scene recreated in the Esplanade Theatre in 1956, by the Bognor Regis
Drama Club.

He remembered that there was more than one Punch and Judy, and he was responsible for employing them. They each had their own 'pitch'. One of the Punch and Judy men had a house in the Steyne and used to store his equipment there and just carry it down the road.

West Sussex Gazette, 22 September 1955 – A Sussex holiday ends: 'You simply cannot take the world too seriously at Bognor Regis. Jets may shriek overhead, but the donkeys still plod along the beach at low tide, and the kind of fun, the holiday crowd loved years ago – from puppet shows and palmists to carriage rides behind horses, and real fishermen in charge of little boats and lobster pots.'

Parade Inspectors

In the 1950s the urban district council employed several parade inspectors and each had their own area to patrol, either along the promenade or in the parks. They were easily recognisable in their uniforms with a peaked cap, so holidaymakers approached them with problems, including reuniting lost children with their parents. Charles said that, with regard to lost children, there were two kiosks opposite the pier. On the west side was the tourist information kiosk and the east-side kiosk housed the St John's (or another similar organization) first-aid post – and it was here that lost children were brought.

He remembers queues of coaches travelling down from Shripney and the east car park being absolutely crammed with these coaches. Alongside the coaches there was the very popular miniature railway, operating from a small station.

Special trains to Bognor Regis from London were organised. There would be a continuous long stream of people walking from the railway station down to the beach.

One of the town's uniformed parade inspectors patrolling the promenade.

The station of the miniature railway adjacent to the East Coach Park at Gloucester Road.

Sidney Briggs ran this extremely popular miniature railway from 1948 to 1952.

Looking at the beach photos and the long stretches of sand and the crowds, he recalled how as the tide came in, people would move further and further back up the beach, onto the lower promenade, then the upper promenade, and they finally spilled over onto the pavement!

Royal Tank Regiment Band

Charles remembers the Royal Tank Regiment Band well as he engaged them for several seasons, and recalls Alan Binns and the Bandleader Lt Bill Lemon – he became friends with him, and Bill and his wife stayed with Charles and his wife on occasions.

The Pier

The pier in Bognor Regis has been a prominent feature since it was opened on 6 May 1865, when it was announced that it was to be 'of a circumstance of such importance to the town of Bognor'.

In 1951 the paddle steamers returned to the pier, adding another layer of entertainment to the seafront.

Charles Powell – Entertainments Manager, Bognor Regis Town Council
Bognor Regis

This is just one of the numerous engines that operated on the pier.

My Summer Job

Whilst many people remember 'someone' diving off the end of the pier, we were lucky to meet someone actually involved in the diving. As with any feature, such as a pier, each generation has used it differently.

The drinking fountain in Waterloo Square in 1955, opposite the pier entrance.

What did the holidaymakers watch when they visited Bognor Regis? They would see me diving off the end of the pier, but they did not know the full story. When I was about 14 or 15 in the mid-1950s a gentleman diver would jump off the end of the pier and he asked my mother if I could join him. She agreed – without asking me – and I joined him. I had to walk to the end of a diving board until my toes went over the end. It was scary as I was then 40ft above the beach. He would then come up behind me and lift me over his head onto his back. Thus my feet would be at the back of his head and I would be laying the length of his spine. I would hang on very tight, and have to tell him when I could actually see the diving board. He would then tell me he was going to jump. The first time, I remember that we seemed to go down and down, and I then had a bit of a panic as to how I was going to get up to the top again. He said next time – there was to be a next time – I should just put my hands down by my side and I would shoot to the surface, which of course I did. He paid me 2/6d (12½p) per jump. He also went around the crowds, collecting, saying the money was to raise money to buy me a bicycle at the end of the season to get to school. Needless to say I never saw the bicycle.

Ruby Knight
Bognor Regis

Press Report

The above activity was not without its hazard and in July 1957 the 40ft plunge was undertaken by 'Tarzan' with a lady on his back but unfortunately, watched by hundreds on the beach, they did not land well and he was rushed to the Bognor Regis Memorial Hospital where he was diagnosed with a dislocated shoulder.

The *Bognor Regis Post*, 21 July 1951 – Underwater thrills at Bognor: An unrehearsed incident momentarily held up a preview performance of Ambrose Smith's aquatic show which opened for the season at the end of Bognor Pier on Wednesday. As one of the young lady performers dived into the 6ft deep and 16ft long glass fronted swimming tank, to open the programme, she lost the strap of her bathing suit. Underwater repairs were quickly effected, and the incident will not be repeated on future programmes!

Eskimo Roll off the Pier

My friend Len Leech and I were both keen kayakers; we were two of only six people who were able to Eskimo roll a kayak in the UK at that time. We had been approached by the British Canoe Union and requested to give demonstrations of kayak rolling in an attempt to bring kayaking to the public eye. We were asked to give these demonstrations on both inland waters and on the coast.

Between 1956 and 1958 we arranged to do demonstrations at the end of Bognor Regis Pier each weekend. These started at Easter and ran to the end of the season. We had no funding to assist us, so in an attempt to minimise our costs we would camp at a farm in South Bersted, the very farm where the speedboats which offered rides from the end of the pier were stored. We would transport our kayaks on a daily basis from farm to pier and then return them to the farm at the end of each day. Our tents were pitched at the beginning of the season and struck at the end of the season. In recognition of the loan of two water suits by Seimens, we would place their products on display. Unfortunately, the suits provided trapped a considerable amount of air making each roll extremely difficult, so they were left on the pier side quite quickly. No doubt they were good for what they were intended for, but not for rolling!

Our kayaks were made of wood and canvas as was usual in the 1950s. Indeed I made my own, with two watertight sections to aid buoyancy. Len's was a professionally made kayak, but still from wood and canvas. This reflected a truer form of an Eskimo kayak than the later glass fibre or indeed spun plastic versions.

The participants in these demonstrations included our wives and children. Len and I worked on the water in rolling our kayaks and performing the odd trick. Len's wife, Pat, would give a running commentary for the spectators who were people visiting the pier. My wife, Janie, would pass round the hat in an attempt to recover some of our costs. Janie recalls once receiving a 10*s* note from a spectator who stated, 'I have never seen anything like it.' My youngest son at the time, Malcolm, aged about 3 years was a boon in encouraging people to donate generously; after all who can resist the imploring looks of a young child!

Our show would start by launching from the limpet encrusted steps that led down from the end of the pier into the water. These steps were frequently the cause of a number of scratches and minor cuts which stung all the more when in the sea! My two older children Carrol and Brian, aged 11 and 9, joined Len and I in the water. They would wrap themselves around the stern and bow of my kayak, imitating seals that had been killed by the Eskimos in their hunting expeditions and then tied onto the kayaks. I would roll my kayak as they both held on tight; sometimes I would roll continuously three or four times. The Eskimos used this rolling technique to save themselves from the freezing waters that would otherwise certainly have killed them.

The idea of a roll is to spin the kayak in a horizontal fashion, but on one occasion I recall a big wave rolled me in the vertical, bow over stern. Fortunately I was not harmed but my kayak required much repair.

Len Leach with John Willis under the upturned kayak.

In addition to the various technical rolls we used to perform some tricks. These included rolling with a top hat and not letting it get wet. Keeping the hat dry involved passing it over both the deck and the keel of the kayak as I would roll. Len would roll and pretend to get stuck; he would then come up in the kayak with a fish in his mouth looking as if he had just caught it. I would also demonstrate how to right a capsized kayak without the use of a paddle. Of course this was a planned demonstration but on one occasion I truly needed this skill as I broke my paddles and this was the only way I could recover myself!

We were fortunate only to need the local St John's Ambulance Service, which was provided opposite the pier entrance, on two occasions. The first time was when I bit into a toffee apple for my son Malcolm as he could not manage it for himself. Unfortunately, just as I bit into the toffee apple a wasp decided to land upon it and got bitten at the same time. The said wasp decided to assert his indignation and stung me on the tongue which led to a greatly swollen tongue which almost stopped me from breathing. The second occasion followed my son Brian's attempt to jump from a beached landing pontoon to the promenade. This resulted in his chin hitting the promenade and sustaining a large and deep cut, indeed he still carries the scar.

A paddle before lunch.

We were not the only people to offer entertainment from the pier or indeed on the beach. My daughter Carrol assisted with the donkeys which offered rides on the beach. She would go to the stables to help in their preparation, bring them to the beach and help with the rides. Then there was a diver who would demonstrate his skills at the pier end, obviously depending upon the tide conditions.

John Willis
London

Theatres

The Pier

Kay Macaulife was very interested in amateur dramatics. She produced and acted in numerous one-act plays for a local theatre group, in Felpham Village Hall. Kay took part in productions of the Phoenix Players, the professional repertory company who performed at the Roof Garden Theatre on the pier in Bognor Regis.

After the Phoenix Players closed, the Buskin Players were formed in 1951. Kay acted in many of their productions during 1951–2, also at the Roof Garden Theatre.

Members of the Buskin Players in 1952 at the Roof Garden Theatre, with Kay Macaulife in the doorway who produced as well as appeared in many of their productions.

ROOF GARDEN THEATRE
BOGNOR REGIS
'Phone: BOGNOR REGIS 575

THE BOGNOR REGIS
REPERTORY THEATRE COMPANY

present

The Importance of Being Earnest
By OSCAR WILDE

Week commencing Mon., June 1, 1953

(Our 191st consecutive week)

Nightly at 8 p.m.

MATINEES—Wednesday at 2.30 p.m., Saturday at 3

Souvenir Programme - - *Price 6d.*

Jennings'—The Printers, West Street, Bognor Regis

A 1953 advertisement for one of the groups who frequented the pier theatres.

The Kursaal/Rex

The Kursaal building was constructed in 1911 on the seafront and was a complete entertainment complex with theatre, ballroom, skating with exterior shops and cafés. (The site today is the Regis public house.) After the Second World War the building underwent an extensive refurbishment in 1947 and reopened under the name of the Rex Entertainment Centre and the theatre was renamed the Theatre Royal as a cinema.

A Dance Hall

The Rex Ballroom was situated at the seaward end of the 'Kursaal' as it was originally called. After the sad demise of the Pavilion dance hall, the Rex became the centre for the meeting of the young (and older) people of Bognor Regis. Many a married couple in Bognor first met at the Rex (as indeed I did). On the way to the Rex we would often meet up at the Sussex Hotel for a few drinks (Dutch courage!) before entering the exciting hall with dreams and anticipation.

The ballroom was a splendid circular hall with a surrounding balcony from where one could sit and survey the talent (boys and girls). The floor was usually packed and not very good for ballroom dancing, but very good for getting introduced.

The floor was always cleared when the wonderful Romaine twins were jiving. Then the dancers would form a circle and applaud as Johnny and Pauline performed. It was a wonderful exhibition. The twins were very well known in the town, helping their mother run the stalls along Bognor Regis seafront.

From the dance floor we went down a couple of ornate stairs to the long bar and then, in the summer, out on the balcony overlooking the sea. What bliss!

The impressive Rex building viewed from York Road, showing various local shops.

The interior of the Rex building hosting a dinner for 150 people.

When the dance finished, usually at about midnight, there was a mad scramble to catch the waiting buses such as the 31 to Middleton and Elmer, 55 to Bersted and 51 (I believe) to Pagham. Nobody had a car then, and it meant a long walk back if you were taking a girl home!

Wonderful place – wonderful days.

Ken Scutt
Bognor Regis – U3A

Holiday Job

I remember my summer job in 1951 when I was 15 years old. In the school holidays I went to work for Tom Boothman at the Rex. I, along with other 15 year olds, worked at laying up and waiting on tables for 1s (5p) per hour.

The Rex had a long room on the first floor which acted as ballroom, a table tennis tournament area and a large dining room set up with trestle tables and chairs.

Large groups visiting Bognor Regis by train on day trips could book in advance for lunch and tea. We were busy at the weekends and worked as casuals during the week as and when they had bookings. Train groups could be up to 500 or 600 people.

Wendy Roberts making friends with a dog on the beach.

The young girls' role was to lay up the tables for lunch. Lunch was always a set meal of meat and three vegetables, a pudding and cold drink. At teatime it would be sandwiches, assorted cakes and tea. It was very hard work but I enjoyed it, especially when it was large groups of children.

Mary Streeter
Bognor Regis

Beach Activities

The beach attracts many people with a variety of memories. We did all the usual things on the beach: digging sandcastles, making pools so that they filled with water when the sea came in, hunting for coloured pebbles and seaweed to decorate our castles, etc. We also played bat and ball and some sort of cricket with other children we met on the beach. We had large balls that you blew up and we would play a game over the breakwater with them.

During the evening we always went out for a walk along the front, ending up in the Butlin's amusement arcade. Here we spent our pennies in the slot machines. Sometimes we went on the pier and watched people fishing. If we were lucky we got treated to a milkshake in a Milk Bar which had tall stools for sitting up to a counter, and was between our boarding house and the pier, before going back to bed. I cannot remember there ever being a sitting room (no TV then), it was just your bedroom or the dining room for meals. One holiday my father bought me a subscription to Boots Children's Library. I think it must have been poor weather, and it gave me something to do, as I could change my book every day! We weren't very far from the park, and sometimes we would go there for a walk. I think it was there they had large Disney-like characters dotted around the grass.

In later years we came to Bognor Regis by car and parked in a large field at the west end of the promenade*. I cannot find it now, so it must have been built on since then. It had a large row of trees between the sea and the field, and wasn't that far to walk to the sea. Here we met our relatives from Crawley and had lovely family days out on the beach. We were very self-sufficient. We brought all our own food and had a little stove for making tea. I don't think we went much further than the beach and the car, but my sister, Betty, who was courting then, would bring her boyfriend and they used to go off for walks and wouldn't let me go with them! Our car wasn't very big (a pre-war Standard 10). It didn't really have room for three people on the back seat, so I had a hassock on the floor between their feet.

*Authors' Note – this would be West Park.

Just one of the seafront entertainments available to visitors.

Bognor Regis was also a favourite place for our Sunday school outings. Attendance at Sunday school rose as the outing came nearer, as you had to have a good number of ticks in the register to qualify for a place on the coach.

For many children it was the only time they got to go to the seaside, so it was a much-prized event, and the coach was always full. In the early 1950s the coaches were quite old and low powered, and when it got to Bury Hill all passengers would have to get out and walk up the hill so the coach could grind its way up to the top! I don't think it went much faster than the walkers.

The tide always seemed to be out and there was lots of sand available for games, etc. (Perhaps the week was chosen with the tide in mind!) Team games were organised and everybody joined in. Swimming was always before lunch and games afterwards.

We had to take our own sandwiches for lunch but were bought a 3*d* ice cream for afterwards.

After the games we would be taken along the front for a walk and allowed to spend our pocket money in the amusement arcade. We were organised into groups of about four children to either one older child helper or an adult (probably the naughty boys were in the charge of an adult!) We were not allowed to stray far on our own, so that there were no missing persons at the end of the day.

Buckets full of fun.

At the end of the afternoon we were taken to a church hall where we were given orange squash or tea with biscuits and cake. This must have been organised by our church with the helpers of the local church in Bognor Regis. It wasn't very far to walk from the front to the church hall, but I cannot remember which one gave us this hospitality. This also provided a good place for using the toilet before getting back on the coach to come home.

Lyn Baily
Middleton-on-Sea, Bognor Regis

Stuck in the Mud

It was 1950 and I went to Bognor Regis with my parents, their two friends Bob and Rose, plus their daughter, Margaret. A sea trip in a motorboat was decided. We all got on board and waited for it to fill up. Unfortunately by the time it was full the tide had started going out. The captain told us the boat was stuck in the sand so he couldn't move it, and we would all have to climb out and paddle across to another boat further out. We took off our footwear and proceeded to paddle across to the other boat. Rose, who was quite short, was trying to keep her skirt up out of the water while Bob was trying to keep it modestly down, when suddenly she stepped into a hole which had been dug in the sand and she went up to her waist. Well, naturally us kids were in hysterics. Suddenly Mum shouted to my dad, 'Look George.' He'd been carrying his sandals and hadn't noticed that he'd dropped one and it was floating out to the sea. By then it was too much for everyone – we couldn't reach the other boat and decided to give up. As we turned around all the people on the beach were laughing. We never did get a boat trip but we did have a lovely holiday in Bognor Regis – and Dad did recover his sandal.

Maureen Carter, *née* Longley
Horsham

A day to remember for Maureen's family.

Shopping on the Prom

In the 1930s my parents opened the well-known Goodacres store situated on the corner of York Road and the promenade. Around 1952 I started working in the shop, which had many facets to it. Downstairs was the parquet floor that lots of people remember and it was here that you could purchase your toys, buckets and spades, etc. We also had teddy bears in a glass cabinet for sale.

Along the promenade side of the shop we also sold cigarettes and newspapers. During the summer months we would get lots of people coming from the coach trips that came into the town. Upstairs the shop stocked the larger toys such as scooters and slides and also prams and pushchairs.

Finally there was another section to the rear of the shop and this was where I worked. Next door to our store, Edith Sparks had a wool and haberdashery shop. When she closed we took over that premise and included it into our shop, which meant two steps down from the main area. It was here that I sold a lot of the fancy goods, the small pieces of china that had Bognor Regis printed on them, to take home as souvenirs to remind the visitors of their holiday to our town.

Pauline Edwards
Bognor Regis

Pauline Goodacre behind the counter of the family business, serving souvenirs and fancy goods to holidaymakers.

Boats

For me, the most exciting sight was if there was a spell of bad weather when Ron Whittington's speedboats *Miss Magic*, *Zip* and *Miss Bognor Regis* and the launches *Sea Hawk* and *Bounty* would have to leave Bognor where there is no harbour and run for shelter at Littlehampton and enter the harbour with all the crews absolutely drenched.

Adrian Collyns
London

The Butlin's zoo on the seafront used to smell of pepper, I don't know if it was because of the various animals inside or not. There were monkeys, a glass maze, ghost train and much more. There was a large spider's web which made us all scream. Along the road was another site which had bumper cars, bingo and a penny arcade. There was a large clown's head that would move side to side, as you put a ball in the mouth.

Sylvia Olliver
Bognor Regis

All aboard for a boat ride.

Deckchairs

The seafront had a wide range of restaurants and cafés for people to use, and in 1953 Macari's opened their restaurant on the Esplanade.

In 1958–9 I was a student and worked on the deckchairs during the summer holidays. The deckchairs were stacked at intervals along the promenade from Gloucester Road to Park Road. There were five stacks and the two largest of about 800 chairs each were just to the east of the pier and opposite the Rex Ballroom at the end of York Road. The chairs were provided by the local council and were all stamped with BRUDC, which was the Bognor Regis Urban District Council.

Peter restacking deckchairs at the end of a busy day during his summer holiday job.

In the 1950s it was necessary to queue to hire a deckchair.

Deckchairs were very popular in those days. I think because people dressed more formally, men often wearing suits and women summer dresses, so obviously they wouldn't want to spoil their clothes by sitting on the beach. A lot of these people were what we called day trippers who came to Bognor Regis for the day either by coach or by train.

Holidaymakers paid a deposit for a chair which we handed to them from the stack and they had their deposit refunded when they returned the chair. We were mostly students and there were also some retired people who usually handed out the tickets. At the end of the day we had to check the beach for any chairs that hadn't been returned and then sheet up the stack with tarpaulins and rope them down in case we had rain or gales.

I often worked on the stack by the Esplanade Theatre. Along the Esplanade was a row of chairs by the rails with sun canopies and also upright folding chairs which were looked after by another person. At times of high tide when the beach was covered, people had to put their chairs on the promenade. In those days, there was a lower promenade as well, which is now buried beneath the shingle.

Peter Tompkins
Bognor Regis

The Fashionable '50s

For the first time, in the '50s young people (i.e. teenagers) had spending power and clothes were being designed specifically targeted at them. Gone were the days when young people were dressed in the same style of clothing as their parents.

This inevitably brought about a major change in wearing clothes for different occasions – none more so that holidaying as, again, young people wanted specific clothing, not content with the same clothes they went to work in.

One of the major changes was in beachwear; the bikini made its first entrance in the early '50s with Brigitte Bardot being the perfect body to display the scant

Relaxing on the lower promenade steps we see (left to right) Gwen, with Wendy her sister-in-law, her mother-in-law and brother Roy.

two-piece – which was definitely not designed for swimming. This era also saw the wearing of flip-flops, initially for the beach but incorporated into casual wear generally.

Young Women

Women started wearing jeans and pedal pushers which had been influenced by cinema and seeing 'bobby-soxers' from USA. Also young women were beginning to wear trousers as part of their lifestyle, which had been frowned upon in earlier years. Dirndl cotton skirts were evident and worn with t-shirts or blouse for holidaying.

Young Men

The male was not left behind – in fact this was one of their most stylish eras.

Teddy boy drape suits with drainpipe trousers started to become fashionable. Also the 'mods' and 'rockers' evolved during this time – both were very recognisable in their particular style.

They also began congregating in seaside towns travelling there on Lambrettas or motorbikes.

Jeans were also beginning to be worn other than for workwear.

However, many young males were not willing to give up their smart suits and ties to go on holiday. They didn't embrace the beachwear as readily as young women.

Josie Landolt
Bognor Regis – U3A

Bingo

Alan and I got engaged in 1955 and until we got married in 1957, most Sundays in the summer we used to play Bingo on the seafront. We always went to the same stall and got to know the caller very well. We paid 6*d* (2.5p) for a card and we used to save up our prizes to get bigger articles such as blankets, towels, tea-services and cutlery for my bottom drawer. The caller married a girl half his age (but this did not last long) so we were able to take over his furnished flat in Gloucester Road when we got married. Also on a Saturday, when Alan left work, we would go to Pat's Pantry, one of the little shops on the station forecourt, where I always had a delicious mushroom omelette. There were only four tables in the café.

Gwen Twaites
Bognor Regis

Youngsters

Ann and Roy in 1955 strolling along the prom.

After being laid up with a bad back for several months, my new fiancé Roy decided that we should have a day out in Bognor Regis. We then rode down on our motorcycle to Bognor Regis. Like many others we would stroll along the prom and we were captured by the seafront photographer on 16 August 1955 as in this snap. Within twelve months Roy and I were married and following other visits we eventually came to live in Bognor Regis in 1988 permanently.

Ann Manville
Bognor Regis

The Ice-Cream Seller

I spent a vacation selling ice cream on the promenade in Bognor Regis, encountering paper-capped, candy-floss-sucking day trippers all day long. During the course of the day I found that many of the customers proved incapable of reading the clearly printed price list. Customers also seemed unable to understand the quaint terms: strawberry, vanilla, cornet or wafer. Some people even asked us the correct way to eat an ice-cream cone. The kiosk itself was quite small – only 10ft by 8ft – and advertised only ice creams for sale; however, people continually asked for cigarettes, magazines or trays of tea for the beach. Being situated so close to the beach we were constantly bombarded with questions about tide times, train times, shopping hours, hotels and cures for sunburn.

Small children were sweet; with solemn faces they would hold up a penny and ask for a 6*d* cone (it was often difficult to refuse). Or, proffering a warm and sandy shilling, order, 'Please Miss a frepenny lolly and some change.' The ice cream sold was from Sait's, manufactured in Chichester 8 miles away. With the factory being

Hazel Macaulife, in her 1955 vacation, serves Sait's ice cream from the kiosk on the Esplanade.

so near and there being a dairy of the same name in Bognor Regis, customers regarded our ice cream as home-made. 'Ooh, Flossie, this is where they sell it home-made,' we would hear outside the kiosk. The customers would then say, 'You make it yourselves, don't you dear?'

Hazel K. Bell, *née* Macaulife
Hatfield, Herts

Diving Platform

Many people remember using the diving raft so it was with interest that we found a report in the local press on 27 May 1950, which gave us a full picture of this well-loved facility:

> The diving raft which has now been anchored opposite the Esplanade Concert Hall has already found great popularity with bathers, and is, I feel, something which has long been needed to improve Bognor's bathing facilities, which previously did not allow for diving.
>
> It is a pity, though, that there is only the one raft. It is going to mean that the groyne off which it is anchored is going to be unduly crowded, and many of the daytrippers who normally confine themselves (by some unwritten law) to the east side of the Pier will doubtless flock to this stretch of beach. At least one diving raft, if not two, should have been provided to the east of the Pier, and many residents would welcome another raft farther to the west.

Charles Powell recalled floodlit bathing from the pontoon – he instigated it himself! The pontoon was moored just off the Esplanade Theatre, which supplied electricity for the lights via a cable. It was open till 11 p.m. and was very popular.

Cafés

As a child I lived in Nyetimber and didn't go into Bognor Regis much, as my friends and I used to play locally either on the beach or cycle around the area, especially to Pagham Lagoon.

My school, the Villa Maria, was in Bognor Regis so I travelled daily by bus and was aware of the seafront and promenade. Also my mother would take me with her when shopping in Bognor Regis, which always included a drink in the Polly Anne Café or, for a treat, a visit to Leslie's Café.

It wasn't until I began work and also started taking evening classes for speed shorthand that I feel I got to know Bognor Regis. Not having time to get home after work and back into Bognor Regis, I needed to find somewhere to go. Not particularly wanting to go where I did with my mother, I found the ice-cream parlour on the corner of Lennox Street and the Esplanade. I think that ice-cream parlours were new to Bognor Regis and they were becoming popular with the younger people (teenagers). They had a relaxed atmosphere where you could meet your friends and not be expected to rush out.

They offered coffees, milkshakes and ice-cream sodas. Also fancy ice-cream sundaes in little silver dishes and also knickerbocker glories.

In the early evening I would sit mainly on my own with a coffee as it was a quiet period, but if a friend and I went there later in the evenings it was always busy. In 1953 a second ice-cream parlour was opened further along the Esplanade called Macari's.

Margaret Richards
Aldwick, Bognor Regis

The Guinness Clock

The original Guinness clock appeared at the 1951 Festival of Britain. It stood 25ft high and its internal mechanism was highly elaborate, which included nine reversible electric motors and three synchronous clocks. Enquiries poured in from many quarters for events, exhibitions and seaside towns to borrow the clock for a display. This inspired Guinness to build eight smaller travelling clocks, plus one miniature of 5ft high. The first two were ready by September 1952 and one went to Morecombe as a main feature of the town's illuminations. The other went to Southend as part of their seaside illuminations. The clocks then toured seaside towns for the next seven years, including coming to Bognor Regis to an area near the Eastern Bandstand.

The Guinness Clock.

EAST AND WEST

Whilst this book is primarily focused on Bognor Regis, we should not forget the adjacent villages, which were just as important for visitors. For this reason we are recording the memories of the visitors who stayed there, many of who would not necessarily travel into Bognor Regis.

Felpham & Middleton-On-Sea

From London
These recollections were told to Helen Krarup by Marilyn Paton.

Marilyn's family has had connections with Bognor Regis since the 1930s. Her grandparents had a building firm in London and owned two houses and a building plot in Elmer as they intended to retire to Bognor Regis. One of the houses was let out to summer visitors.

Marilyn and her brother and parents lived in London but came to Bognor Regis frequently to clean her grandparent's cottage between rentals. The family travelled down from London by car – often at bedtime – in their black Austin with running boards. They would be put straight to bed when they arrived. Marilyn describes her childhood as being a great contrast between living in London and experiencing all that London offered during the week, and spending idyllic free, enjoyable days in Bognor Regis on holidays and many weekends during the summer.

She and her brother would roam the fields and beaches, and spent many hours playing on the empty plot next door; they always had a rope to swing on the trees in the plot. They wore their old clothes and climbed trees, pretending to be The Famous Five with the children who lived next door and their dog – Marilyn was George and her brother had to be Ann as no one else would be! They built tree houses and had wonderful freedom; they never felt as if they had a lot but they did. They all used to play outside in the street and spent hours making and firing arrows and were always out in the sunshine; Marilyn's dad was always doing something on the plot, around the house, etc. They used to spend lots of time on the beach, swimming and playing as a family.

Sea erosion was always a problem. There was a hotel named the Villa Plage and many more attractions. There was the Candy Store where they often went for ice creams. There was no fast food or anything like that, so they just took their own food to the beach where they met up with other kids. She talked about building sandcastles and sand cars facing the sea – using the tide to pretend to drive the cars. They took their own deckchairs and would go for the day; it was always busy. Elmer beach is now flat but there used to be steps down to it – the sea defences have changed all that. By 1959 the wartime stakes were still on the beach and there was a lot of shingle. She vividly remembers running along the lower prom wall as the tide was coming in. Sometimes they went to other beaches for a change – Angmering for example.

At that time there were many holiday rental properties in Elmer – which was a popular holiday destination, with a number of shops. There were lots of bungalows and some residents but many holidaymakers. A large number of the people who rented were Londoners; they came down all year round, almost every weekend in the summer and for a week before the rental season started.

Marilyn's family went home on Sunday after tea and Marilyn used to pretend to be asleep when they arrived home so she would be carried up to bed. Marilyn described an idyllic childhood by the sea – all homemade but full of fun and enjoyment which clearly meant a lot to her then and still does now.

Marilyn Paton
Felpham, Bognor Regis – U3A

An Idyllic Time

In the 1940s we lived in Fulham, London, but my in-laws had properties in Elmer, around the Layne area. We would come down for holidays, weekends and even over the Christmas period.

Following our life in London, where my husband had his business, he would drive us down late on a Friday evenings to miss the traffic and return to collect us on a Sunday evening.

In the beginning we came down for the weekend to help the in-laws with the cleaning of their holiday accommodation, which was what many of the premises consisted of. In later life many of these holidaymakers returned to the area to retire.

We thought it was an idyllic time. We had all the shops nearby so that we could purchase whatever we required without travelling far, this would then leave us time to go down to the beach, just a stone's throw away. When the children got older they were able to go down to the beach for a swim and leave their shoes on the top of the wooden columns whilst they went into the water to collect later in the day. Memories consist of these quiet times where the children had the freedom to run down to the beach and play unsupervised for hours.

Elmer was a place where many people came to stay in their holiday homes, some of which consisted of just a wooden bungalow with very few rooms and a shingle roof, but this allowed for ideal stays by the beach. The beach at that time was well below the level which it is today and consisted of sand which enabled the children to run around, especially between the various piers and groynes that existed.

The Dixon family on Elmer beach.

Remains of sea defences on Elmer beach.

As we began to have more holidays here, our London friends would regularly ask if they could come down to enjoy the peaceful holidays. Out of all my happy holiday memories in Elmer, the favourite of these is of the Candy House which sold cakes, sweets and Sait's ice creams, always a popular place for all age groups.

Sheila Dixon
Felpham, Bognor Regis

FELPHAM, SUSSEX
(NEAR BOGNOR REGIS)

A QUAINT AND CHARMING VILLAGE—RIGHT ON THE SEA. ITS GLORIOUS SANDS ARE NEVER CROWDED AND THE BATHING IS NOT EXCELLED ANYWHERE IN ENGLAND. THE IDEAL SPOT FOR THOSE SEEKING A "DIFFERENT HOLIDAY," 'MIDST THE NATURAL BEAUTY OF SEA AND DOWNLAND. "FAR FROM THE MADDING CROWD," YET—ONLY 5 MINUTES TO BOGNOR REGIS AND ALL AMENITIES OF MODERN SEASIDE RESORT.

KENWOOD

Stands in half-acre beautiful gardens. Fruit. vegs., poultry, fresh eggs home produced.
Interior Spring Beds. H. & C.
Terms from 5 to 7 Guineas.
S.A.E. for Brochure "G."
Resident Proprietress : Mrs. OLIVE NEARY, "Kenwood," Felpham, Bognor Regis.

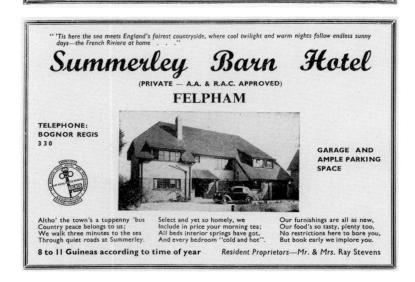

" 'Tis here the sea meets England's fairest countryside, where cool twilight and warm nights follow endless sunny days—the French Riviera at home . . ."

Summerley Barn Hotel

(PRIVATE — A.A. & R.A.C. APPROVED)
FELPHAM

TELEPHONE:
BOGNOR REGIS
330

GARAGE AND
AMPLE PARKING
SPACE

Altho' the town's a tuppenny 'bus	Select and yet so homely, we	Our furnishings are all as new,
Country peace belongs to us;	Include in price your morning tea;	Our food's so tasty, plenty too,
We walk three minutes to the sea	All beds interior springs have got,	No restrictions here to bore you,
Through quiet roads at Summerley.	And every bedroom "cold and hot".	But book early we implore you.

8 to 11 Guineas according to time of year   Resident Proprietors—Mr. & Mrs. Ray Stevens

Advertisement from a 1950 town guide.

Never Bored

We were never bored living here. We all went out on our bikes, largely in and around Felpham. We roamed around the fields and the ditches where the Summerley Fields Estate is now. A circular banked area which may have been an old anti-aircraft gun position was a favourite place. We made model aeroplanes; there was a model shop in Nyewood Lane at West Bognor shops. We used to cycle to Goodwood and Arundel. I have very fond memories of the Esplanade and the theatre on the pier where the Bognor Regis Operatic Society used to put on shows – musicals like *White Horse Inn* and *Brigadoon*. I fell in love with them and much later joined a society and played many parts. That led to occasional professional acting jobs and Equity membership.

I remember funfairs coming to West Park and once a circus came there. The funfair in Felpham was very popular on the King George VI field. I remember roll a penny, the bumper cars were a favourite, candy floss, hoop-la and, of course, the roundabout. There was a kind of romance about the funfair, I thought, in the evening when the lights came on and the girls were there – an ideal teenage flirting ground!

I remember Southdean Holiday Camp, a place where there were chalets on the seafront. It was created from the old Norman Thompson Aircraft factory and had its own entertainment. Lots of holidaymakers just walked about Middleton enjoying the air and the surroundings. The beach was different then, we always had some shingle but not as much as there is now which is similar to Bognor Regis, where the lower part of the promenade is now hidden by the shingle.

Hugh Coster
Felpham, Bognor Regis

Afternoon tea at Felpham. Hazel Macaulife (standing) outside her grandmother's beach hut (left).

Pagham and Rose Green

Situated to the west of Bognor Regis is the area known as Pagham, which has provided holidays over the years, not only in houses but also in caravans and railway carriages. Now, in 2014, when looking at this area we do not appreciate how different it was back in the 1950s.

The Whole Family

I remember the 1950s as our family spent holidays in Pagham. I was an only child but with an auntie and uncle joining my parents, Gran and Granddad, I remember happy family fun.

We usually stayed in railway carriage homes in Pagham but one year we had a bungalow in Lagoon Lane, Pagham, which was great fun as it was on stilts. I and the other children staying nearby would climb down underneath and make camps. We also had a tunnel formed by a mass of shrubs at the back of the bungalow which only children could get through and was therefore magic.

The social cycles* were hired for trips out and our days would end with drinks in the garden of the Lamb Inn. Such happy holidays!

Felicity Mills
Midhurst

*Authors' Note – social cycles had a double seat where two people
sat side by side, each with their own handlebars and set of pedals.
You were sat in an upright position with the pedals in front of you.

Felicity and family holidaying, seen here in front of a railway carriage at Pagham.

The Chemist

We learnt from Daphne Thomas that she and her husband ran the chemist in Rose Green from 1955 to 1975. They were able to tell us that there were only two caravan parks in that area and no other bed and breakfast style of accommodation. There were lots of fields in this area and it wasn't until the late 1950s that the area started to develop. They were always busy with holidaymakers during the season as there was no other chemist in the area.

Family from Frimley

As a family we lived in Frimley (on the Surrey/Hants/Berks border) and, for some years, travelled to Bognor Regis for a week in the summer and once, if I recall correctly, in the Easter holidays.

My father was a sales man for India Tyres so we had a car, which we used to travel to Bognor Regis; this was long before the major trunk roads that now exist so our route was a fairly picturesque one through the Downs. As children we knew we were on the right road when we passed a rather grand house in Hindhead called Twizletwig. We still had a long way to go but, from that point on, all three of us were straining to get the first glimpse of the sea! I was at a disadvantage being the youngest and hence the smallest.

We always stayed at a caravan site in Rose Green run/owned by a man that we called in the family 'Mr Bleach'. It was not his real name, of course, but as close as I was able to get to Mr Leach. I think that his wife and son also were involved

Left to right: Tony Beales, Sandra (Sue) Beales and Sybil Denyer.

11/11/22

Kellen, Roz

Reserved Item(s)

Branch: Eastbourne Library
Date: 27/10/2022   Time: 11:31
Name: Kellen, Roz
ID:

Item: A 1950s holiday in Bognor Regis
         04268073

Expires: 10 Nov 2022

CIVICA

'Springtime' Dark Lane, Aldwick.

in the site's management. I remember that the caravans were always small and a bit primitive and they had gas lights! It was a skill that my parents learned over the years to be able to light them without shattering at least one mantle in the week. But as children we loved it.

One of the first things we 'had' to do when we arrived was get to the seafront in Bognor Regis and find the rock shop so that we could squander (Mum and Dad's view) our pocket money on rock. I always bought a giant humbug. At my young age it was huge! I used to ration myself to licking it for a period each evening (no TV to distract me) and it could last all week. Great care was required in the licking as the black stripes wore away more slowly than the white body and in the process very sharp edges grew that would lacerate my tongue if I was not careful. I was seldom careful enough! My brother and sister always bought a stick of red rock (with Bognor Regis going through) and sucked them into points.

The beach area we usually went to, which we called 'the rocks', was at Pagham. I can't recall exactly where*, but it was approached down a rather dark lane on foot (there being no room to park the car) past a big stone wall and through a long, dark, arch of big trees. We used to guddle (play) in the rock pools and around the breakwaters looking for crabs, and in the sand, when it got exposed, to make castles or moats or big holes.

A young Doug Law (right), sitting with his family at their Copthorne Caravan site.

Our father, being in the tyres trade, used to bring great big inner tubes and he'd inflate them at a garage on the way to Bognor Regis (which made it a bit tight in the car) so that we could play in the sea. In hindsight, that was not in the least bit safe, but we loved it. On one occasion at the rocks, we had either just arrived or were ready to leave, I can't recall which, I was fully dressed and playing on the seawall just above the rocks themselves (and below a small cliff?) when I slipped into the water. I was drenched but we had no spare clothes with us on the beach and none available at the caravan – all dirty I guess. I was stripped to my skin and wrapped in a towel, then on the way back to the caravan my parents bought me a complete set of new clothes. I clearly recall the indignity and shame of standing on the shop counter wearing not even a smile. My father was not a happy man that night!

At the caravan park, where of course it was always sunny, we used to play with whatever other children were there, at tennis (arguing about the rules, as none of us had any real knowledge of them) and also football (ditto on rules) and as a real treat we flew the kite. Well actually we hardly ever managed to fly the kite as the wind was always too light (as I said the weather was always good) and the kite was not the best. It was a box kite the same size as me, with aluminium struts and linen cloth. By today's standards it was very heavy and not aerodynamic. That said, I still enjoy flying kites and so does my son and his daughter – it must be genetic.

Doug Law
Camberley – U3A

*Authors' Note – this was Dark Lane.

A Chittering Bite

Doug Law's sister recalled that they went to find a change of clothes for Doug and all of the shops were closed except for the little drapery-cum-everything shop just before the entrance to the Bleach's caravan park, on the left approaching the park gate.

I remember that Mum and Dad would say we could go to the beach on our own and they would catch up later. There was no 'stranger danger' then! Apparently no fear of drowning either, or maybe they hoped we would!

It was very cold at times, but it didn't stop us going into the water. We probably knew we would get a 'chittering bite' (a Scottish expression meaning a snack – I think), when mum arrived. We would say, 'Come on in Mum, please, please. It's not that cold,' through blue lips and chattering jaws. We knew that if we could persuade her it would be more fun and then we might get to stay longer. I remember changing under a towel. I am glad that I never had to wear again the hand knitted cozzy that mum had made and that stretched down to my ankles when I went into the water. It got waterlogged and was ugly.

We went to the pictures if it rained and what a treat that was. I remember the argument with two old ladies who had taken our allocated seats in the cinema and Dad rushing us all out after one said, in her imperious voice, 'But we *always* have these seats on a Wednesday.' Dad didn't wait to argue that it was Tuesday. We were disappointed and the fact that it was Tuesday was not uttered in Dad's presence.

Sheena Cribb,
Riverhills, Brisbane, Australia

Aldwick

Richmond to Richmond

I can remember coming to Bognor Regis in 1950 for my holidays with my mum and dad and my younger sister Gillian, when I was 7 years old. I felt very lucky as many of my friends only had a week's holiday, some had none and our family had two weeks, which was very rare. I always remembered where we stayed because it was in Richmond Ave, West Bognor Regis; our home was Richmond in Surrey.

We usually remained in this area, using the small shops on the corner of Nyewood Lane and Aldwick Road. Each day we played on the beach in front of the Marine Park Café (in 2014 The Waverley). We built sandcastles and went shrimping, being joined by Aunt Kath and Uncle Bill and my two cousins, Joan and Peter, who stayed in a caravan at Church Farm in Pagham.

For a treat we would be taken as far as the pier, where we were allowed to pay our money at the booth at the entrance for a ride on the miniature train. If the tide and winds were right we had great fun watching a man dive off the end of the pier.

Jennifer and Gillian with their mother on the shelter roof in Marine Park Gardens.

The toyshop where Jennifer and Gillian bought their kite is seen on the left.

Marine Park Cafe & Restaurant

WEST PARADE, BOGNOR REGIS

Adjoining the Marine Park Gardens and Facing the Sea
With own Car Park

| *Morning Coffee* | :: | *Luncheons* | :: | *Teas* |

CATERING FOR PARTIES   MAY WE QUOTE YOU

A 1954 town guide advertisement.

A joint effort by Jennifer and Gillian with a friend.

Another of our favourite treats after our evening meal was when we all went to the Marine Park Gardens where we played on the putting green.

Our usual route from our accommodation to the beach was down Nyewood Lane, and Gillian and I loved to look in to the toy shop next to the Marine Park Café. One windy day when we arrived at the beach the tide was right in so Dad took us into the toy shop. He said we could choose a kite which we spent a time selecting and we then all went onto the promenade and had a great time flying it.

My most exciting memory was one afternoon when we all went to the Esplanade Theatre to watch the children's talent contest. By the middle of the show I'd plucked up the courage to go up on the stage, but I couldn't think of what to sing. Then I remembered, 'I've got a lovely bunch of coconuts'. To my surprise I won a prize, which was a Mobo pony with pedal chariot, the size children could ride in. I think I remember that was the year the theatre had a Mobo promotion. I can vividly remember the problems of not only getting it back to the accommodation, but also getting it back to Richmond. This was the only competition I entered in Bognor Regis.

Jennifer Jennings, *née* Steel
Bognor Regis

A LINE FROM BOGNOR REGIS.

Messages from Bognor Regis.

A WARM WELCOME AWAITS YOU AT BOGNOR REGIS

And Finally

And finally, one we just couldn't leave out.

In the *Bognor Regis Post* of 25 May 1957 it reports that Mrs Ellen Lingley, aged 83, came on holiday to Bognor Regis with a group of old-aged pensioners. She was given a special greeting by the chairman of the council. Why? Well it was the first time she had seen the sea and in fact her first holiday. Her reactions on her first view – 'I never dreamt it was all water! It's so shiny! And the way it burst against the town, it's a terrible sensation it doesn't seem right.' Her first afternoon was spent in a deckchair on the promenade just looking at the English Channel.

As the 1950s faded and we welcomed in the 1960s, Bognor Regis appeared well placed to continue being one of the favourite seaside resorts on the South Coast.

If you enjoyed this book, you may also be interested in …

Butlin's: 75 Years of Fun!

SYLVIA ENDACOTT & SHIRLEY LEWIS

This nostalgic selection of images illustrates the history of the various camps and hotels of Butlin's. From Redcoats to water worlds, and from the Glamorous Grandmothers competitions to National Talent contests, this book provides an enjoyable and nostalgic trip down memory lane for all who know and love this quintessential British holiday.

978-0-7524-5863-2

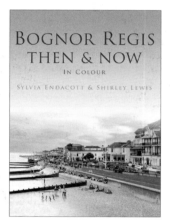

Bognor Regis Then & Now

SYLVIA ENDACOTT & SHIRLEY LEWIS

Delving deep into the town's past, *Bognor Regis Then & Now* compares forty-five rare archive photographs of the town over the last 200 years to the same scenes of today. From Hotham Park House and The Ship Inn to the Esplanade Theatre and Waterloo Square, this title captures the essence of the town and its people.

978-0-7524-8284-2

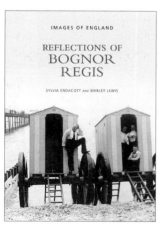

Reflections of Bognor Regis

SYLVIA ENDACOTT & SHIRLEY LEWIS

Bognor Regis is today a thriving but relaxing seaside resort. Illustrated with over 200 images this fascinating book depicts the growth and changes to the town and its surrounding villages from its earliest origins up to the 1970s, and shows the people and the buildings that have made Bognor Regis what it is today.

978-0-7524-4299-0

Visit our website and discover thousands of other History Press books.

www.thehistorypress.co.uk